In the Quiet Season

and other stories

In the Quiet Season

and other stories

Martha Amore

UNIVERSITY OF ALASKA PRESS, FAIRBANKS

Published by
University of Alaska Press
P.O. Box 756240
Fairbanks, AK 99775-6240

Cover and interior design by Kristina Kachele Design, llc

Cover image *Winter Walk*, mixed media, 2016, by Indra Arriaga.

Library of Congress Cataloging in Publication Data

Names: Amore, Martha, author.
Title: In the quiet season : and other stories / Martha Amore.
Description: Fairbanks, Alaska : University of Alaska Press, 2018. |
Identifiers: LCCN 2017026671 (print) | LCCN 2017032183 (ebook) |
ISBN 9781602233539 (ebook) | ISBN 9781602233522 (softcover : acid-free paper)
Classification: LCC PS3601.M6655 (ebook) | LCC PS3601.M6655 A6 2018 (print) |
DDC 813/.6dc23

LC record available at https://lccn.loc.gov/2017026671

For my mother, who was a great reader

Contents

IN THE QUIET SEASON

We hadn't gathered driftwood together all season, but Tara suggested it after lunch and so we hunted down the old orange toboggan and the little gas chainsaw from the side shed. It was cold in the way Fairbanks is in January, fragile with frost, when it seems that even blowing on the trees will crack them to the ground. On the drive to the river access, Tara stared out the window like she was searching for something, her eyes not just scanning all that white landscape but studying it, memorizing it, as if her life depended on every stunted spruce.

"Ted," Tara said, shifting in her seat, "I don't want things to be weird anymore, okay? It's Saturday. I just want a nice time at the river, and then we go back to the cabin and cook up the caribou roast, maybe open a bottle of wine. Okay?"

I drummed my gloved fingers on the steering wheel to the sound of Neil Young on the radio. A raven swooped down, catching a draft of air from the car in front of us. I kept thinking it would fly off, but it stayed there, beating its wings, determined to lead us down the road.

"Okay," I said.

"Really? Okay?"

Tara was always asking for reassurance these days. How did I know if it would be okay? Last winter, after fifteen years of our marriage, Tara cheated on me. She was unfaithful. She met him at a schoolteacher conference down in Anchorage and came home crying, begging my forgiveness. For a long time we lived as strangers. Worse, we lived as though the other wasn't there. Ours was a small cabin, and it took a lot of effort to keep our bodies from touching, our eyes from meeting.

"Okay means okay," I said.

She didn't look convinced but said no more about it.

We watched the raven play on its current of air. His wing feathers fanned out, his body rising up and up, then the fans snapped shut in a dive.

"This bird is having the time of his life," Tara said.

"What I'd do if I could fly."

During spring breakup, Tara and I started having more to do with one another, talking about day-to-day things like the hundred bucks we had to send to the dentist, how the truck was making that rattle noise again, and look, the swallows are back in the eaves—that sort of thing.

Last month Tara started seeing a therapist. She got on me to go with her, and I did. I went with her once. The shrink was an old-timer with big coffee-stained teeth and plugs of gray hair in his nose. Tara cried a lot. She told the old man everything, all about the miscarriages—four in five years— and how alone she felt living at the ends of the earth with no family near and me out at jobsites most of the time. He nodded his big head again and again. Then he turned to me. "Can you describe what you feel right now, in this moment, sitting and listening to your wife?" He leaned over his gut and fixed his watery eye on me. I went mute. My lips felt strange and stiff. I didn't know how to arrange my face or where to look. "I'm just here," I finally said. Best I could do. He must have thought so too because he let me be the rest of the session.

Right at the end, though, the old man took me aside and said something that stuck. I've been turning it around in my mind ever since. *People think the game is all about love, but that's not true. The game is trust. Work on trust.*

"I can't believe this bird is still at it," Tara said.

It was strange how long he coasted in front of us. Oil black against the white road.

"Remember that raven who hung around the summer we built the cabin?" she said. "I finally got him to take granola right out of my palm?"

"Yeah. I remember."

I couldn't help but smile. We built the cabin together way back when Tara was new to Alaska. She was a sight, in her tight jeans and tank top, pounding nails. She came from New York City, and I was surprised by how simple she liked things. Bathing with nothing but a bucket and my grubby blue bandana, cooking dinners on the Coleman or over the burn barrel, and she not only tolerated the outhouse, she jigged a moon, sun, and stars into the door. Best in the neighborhood, that outhouse.

We made love at night and coffee in the morning, and I knew that was how it would always be.

I glanced at her now. The winter cold had burned the center of her cheeks, and she looked healthy, still a beautiful woman. I felt the old rushing within me, and almost laid my hand on her knee. But just as quick, the moment passed. A sharp sliver of hurt took up its old position, left me choking like I had a salmon bone lodged in my throat.

Tara knew it, too. Her smile faded, and she laid her head against the seat.

We drove on in silence. The raven wavered on its air current, gliding up and down, every so often rising on a powerful flap, and then—maybe a change in draft?—it tilted a wing and in a snap was gone.

I parked the truck in a small empty lot enclosed by a high berm. Dropping the tailgate, I hauled out our gear, and when I turned, Tara was way over by the frozen river, surveying up and down the bend. There was no wind, and her vaporized breath hung above her like smoke. There was nothing, not a sound, all along the river valley. The quiet season, what my dad used to call this time of year.

We made down for the river and then continued on, following snow machine tracks single file with me in front. I was going at a good clip. The sun never far above the horizon this time of year, we didn't have much more than an hour at best. Pretty soon, I realized I'd overdressed, sweat dripping from my armpits down to my waist, my long johns soaking through.

I was thinking about what the old man said. Maybe love is cheap in a sense. I mean cheaper than trust. There are a thousand ways to love: love for your mother, love for your neighbor, love for the coffee girl who never remembers your name, love for your dog, love for the way two pieces of wood come together at the first cut. Love can be wide, a feeling you have welling up in you with no one person or thing to settle it on. But trust is tricky. It depends on another. I trust *you* with my life. Learn to trust *one another*. In *God* we trust. But what is it we're giving away when we trust? And what do we hope for in return? Protection? Is that it? Protection from harm? Is the root of trust fear? What the hell does trust mean?

"Wait," Tara called.

Her down hood up, a balaclava wrapped around her mouth, all I could make out were her big brown eyes, the lashes white with frost. She pointed to a trail in the powder.

I was suffocating in the big parka. I unzipped it past my chest. "Porcupine," I said.

"I love these tracks. You can't even see any footprints, just a tunnel in the snow."

"They're too fat. Why they taste so good."

"Can't we for once just enjoy nature without talk of *eating* it?"

Her age-old complaint about me. Pretty smile lines jumped to the corners of her eyes.

We found a good log, and the chainsaw jerked to life in my hands. I cut while she piled the dry wood into the sled. Good thing about driftwood is no waiting, you can burn it the same season. We took the load to the truck and then set out to find more, following a different set of snow machine tracks downriver.

Another log, half frozen into the bank. We sat down on it and passed the Nalgene back and forth. A chill crept up my chest, and I zipped the parka. "We can take off the end of this one," I said. I tossed my gloves next to the sled. "Ready?"

"As ever."

The trunk had lots of branches, and I cut them away first, then got set for the big cuts. I had a chill now and wished to hell I hadn't overdressed in the first place.

I eased the saw into the far end of the trunk, and a good-sized log dropped into the snow. Tara grappled with it for a minute and then got a good grip and hoisted the fresh cut into the sled.

"Atta girl!"

She stopped and put hands on her hips, the smile lines back again. "This is something new."

"I've been hauling wood since I was in diapers."

She pulled the balaclava from her mouth. "You know what I mean."

Just then I got her meaning, and I swallowed down hard on the hurt choking me. If she had only let us go on hauling wood without calling attention to everything little thing like it was a sign. But here we were again. I shrugged.

She looked at me and shook her head.

"What?" I said, more like a curse than a question.

"No matter what I say or do or how much time passes, it just doesn't matter, does it? From here on out, this is how it will be? This is how you want it?"

I revved the chainsaw and made a slow, satisfying cut.

She was yelling over the sound of the saw, and I made another cut. Then another.

Then something ugly reared in me. I turned the saw off, threw it on the ice, and said, "Ask the fucking schoolteacher how he wants it. Go on and ask him. Have your miscarriages with him."

The silence on the river was absolute. I threw my head back and blinked hard to loosen the ice in my lashes. My fingers had gone numb, and I shook them like rags.

"Where *are* you?" she whispered.

I bent and fumbled with the last section of log, my hands useless now and so I held it between my forearms. Tara stood there, chin tucked, arms clamped across her chest, her body closed against the cold. Part of me wanted to go to her and hold her, and tell her *I'm so sorry. I'm so sorry. Anything you want*. But that's not what I did.

I pointed up, and said, "Getting late," although the sky was much brighter than where we stood. Darkness spreads first from the woods, the sky always last to go black.

Tara grabbed the rope, gave it a violent shake, and went on ahead pulling the sled. I had a mind to just sit down in the snow and let her go, but my feet crunched along behind her as if they had their own agenda. For some reason, I started thinking of this game all about opposite words that Tara used to play with me before her students took their big state tests. She'd say something like, *Day is to night as harangue is to?* And I'd rattle off *polar bear piss* or whatever nonsense popped into my head, just to make her laugh. Plus, lots of times I didn't have a clue as to what the word meant. Now, with each step, this phrase kept running through my mind: *Love is to hate as trust is to? Love is to hate as trust is to? Love is to hate as trust is to?*

We were almost back to the access when she came to a stop and turned back to me.

"Do you hear that?"

For a second I thought maybe I'd been talking out loud. But when I stopped and listened to all that winter quiet, I did hear something. It was a sound like a giant insect might make. And there it was again.

We climbed up the bank and peered into the trees. Something big and dark moved quickly, straight up and down.

"Holy shit," I said.

Tara crept closer to the stand. "I think it's some kind of bird."

We moved between the branches to where the creature lay. "It's an eagle!"

Immature but still a giant. Sometimes you see them in the summer but never this time of year. One wing spread out along the white snow, stretching several feet, and when it swept up and down, the air fanned our faces. The snow was stained red under the wing.

"It's hurt," Tara said, moving in.

"Watch out!" I pulled her back.

She shrugged out from under my hand. As she bent over the enormous dark bird, the wing beat once more, but that was it. The eagle just lay in the snow. Its head did not rise, though its cold eye tracked Tara's movements.

"She's a goner," I said.

"No. Maybe not." Tara reached a hand down to touch the bird, and the wing moved once again, more slowly.

"I wouldn't do that."

And then Tara was taking off her parka.

"What are you doing?"

"I'll wrap her and we can take her to the pet emergency or wherever."

"Pet emergency? No. What the hell are they gonna do? No way. That bird is huge. Look at those talons."

She squatted down and eased her parka over it. "We're not far from the truck."

"Look, we can call Fish and Game when we get back home."

"She'll be dead by then."

"That's nature."

But Tara was gently wrapping the monstrous bird in her parka. The eagle's head was limp, and that coupled with the intensity in the bird's eyes turned my stomach. There was blood everywhere now. Tara was moving the bird, tucking her coat around it. The red stain in the snow grew bigger and bigger. All along Tara's shoulder, chest, and arms, her white fleece had turned red.

"Help me!"

I kneeled next to her. "My hands are frozen."

Tara had rolled the bird into the parka, and now she held it right up against her chest. Feathers wet with blood stuck to her fleece. Through the bottom of the parka, one wing hung down. I could see torn skin and tiny bones laid open in the cold.

"This is pointless."

Tara gentled the wing back under her coat and said, "Let's go."

We left the wood and gear on the river, and I pulled Tara with the bird in the sled the short way back to the truck. Feeling burned back into my hands, and I thought I might be sick.

Tara slid onto the bench seat with the bird on her lap and nodded to me to swing the door shut. After, I stood beside the truck, shaking my hands and whispering *goddamn* to the empty parking lot. When I climbed into the truck and started the engine, it startled the bird. She began a sharp chirping and the parka came alive in Tara's lap. Then the bloodied head emerged, and the eagle locked its cold eye on mine.

I shrank back. "Jesus Christ!"

"It's all right," Tara cooed, but whether to the bird or me, I didn't know. "It's going to be all right."

A warm blast from the heater circulated the stench. It smelled no different than downed field game, moose or caribou, a particular scent of iron and fear, and after a while, the bird lay still.

When we arrived at the vet, I opened my door and the bird began to thrash once again. I dashed around to open Tara's door. Streaks of blood and feathers covered her chest and face. "They're not gonna know what to do with this thing," I said.

Talons broke free and sliced Tara's snow pants. She pushed the claw back under the parka with the thick of her mitten. "You're going to have to take her in. My arms are too tired. What you're going to do is lean in, gather all the fabric around her, and hold her tight right up against your body. Don't loosen your hold even for a second."

"What are we accomplishing here, Tara?"

"Take her. Now."

I leaned into the cab, holding my head as far back as possible. The game stench hit me full force, and I thought, *This is what pain smells like.*

And then I was picturing the eagles I see in summer, soaring in gentle circles way up in the bright sky. How could this be the same creature?

"You're doing fine," Tara said.

The bird began to move, pushing against my arms and chest. I instinctively clamped down against her. The closeness of the bird was oddly intimate, and her movements weren't the wild thrashing I'd imagined but rather rhythms that I began to anticipate. It was a sort of dance we were caught up in.

"Come on," Tara said.

I took a step, and then another step. I shifted with the changing dimensions of the bird in my arms. We were too late, and what I held was most certainly going to die, but I went on anyway. I'd never been this close to an eagle before. I stayed circled around the bird until she finally quieted and lay against me. And then I thought, *This is trust.*

GEOLOGY

Geyserites. Black opal. Shale storm. Layers of rock covering the hot liquid core of the planet are more real to her than the ever-shifting human landscape. Once she had broken a bone. No, once a bone had been broken for her. Her stepfather, in a storm and drunk, breaking her arm so that the white bone flashed for just a moment in the earth's long flow of time. Bright white before blood and darkness overcame her.

"My sense of time is all messed up," Kris says soon after we meet.

We are two women at a party full of bearded men, a sprawling Alaska affair with two bonfires, three kegs, and an edgy pack of dogs vying for salmon skin and dominance. My husband left hours ago, and now the cold of freeze-up has driven us into a cavernous garage. The cement floor is slick with beer, and the place smells of yeast and motor oil. A too-loud boy band has her coming in close, yelling her words. I like how she leans into me, her lips occasionally grazing my ear.

"Normal people think in terms of hours, days, weeks. I think in terms of millions of years." A sly smile spreads from her full lips to her dark lashes.

Fine lines, three of them, stretch from the corners of her eyes, which, blue or green, I can't decide. "Lisa," she says, "do you know how old the earth is?"

I squint across the crowded room as though the answer were written on the far wall. The only number that comes to mind is eleven thousand, which is not the age of our planet but the number of wolves in Alaska. I match her smile. "Older than me?"

"What are you, thirty?"

"And then some."

"The planet is a bit older than that." As she speaks, she puts a hand to my hip. "Six billion years. Can you get your mind around that?"

"No."

Her hand stays on me.

Was it the broken arm that saved her life? Finally, a visible wound. Her mother had no choice but to take action and leave her stepfather. No, I think she saved herself. The form of escape she chose, not drugs or self-loathing, but college. Geology.

The first day her professor cast away the syllabus and hefted a cracked-in-half stone. A private universe of bright sherbet lacework lay hidden within the thick gray husk, and at the very center, a hollow the size of a child's fist.

"This is a geode," her professor said, walking up and down the aisle with the cracked stone in his palms. He pointed to the pink crystal ring, "Quartz," and to the spread of pink, "Dolomite." Then he smoothed his finger along the purple streaks of crystal and said, "Amethyst."

When he returned to the podium, she followed, taking the seat before him. "And this?" she asked, indicating the empty core.

Her professor smiled. "Trapped air, perhaps? Or maybe the remains of a small animal burrow?" He looked at her and blinked, his shaggy gray eyebrows matching both the great mane on his head and the hair sprouting from his nostrils. "Imagine with me, miss. Millions of years ago, some minute amount of life found its way into this rock, perhaps bacterium or just a mere trickle of water? And time pressed on and on and on, species of dinosaurs emerging and dying out, the shifting of continents, the birth of countless animal species, including our own. And through it all, there is this rock." He paused, regarded her over the tops of his bifocals, and for the first time in her life, she felt seen by somebody.

"In Iceland," he said, "they say the rocks are alive, that in fact, they have souls."

Years later, when she had completed her graduate thesis, he gifted her the geode, wrapped in red ribbon with a card reading, *A souvenir from the Miocene.*

The musicians take a break. The bearded men stagger from the garage to the bonfires outside, but we remain huddled close, our voices dropping low. A charm is strung around her neck. I reach out for it, a small purple crystal, and my fingers rest against her warm skin. Up close, I see that the crystal is not a solid color, but many different shades ranging from clear to lavender to nearly black.

"Beautiful," I say.

"Amethyst."

We smile at one another. She takes a drink of beer and licks the foam from her lips. I wonder what it would be like to kiss her? What harm is there, I think, in a kiss?

We startle to the noise of the garage door. It opens, revealing the dark night outside. Woodsmoke overpowers the scent of motor oil, and with the rush of cold she shifts her body against mine. I make out black figures around a blazing fire, but their voices carry away into the night. My eyes adjust, and in the moonlight there are the jagged white tips of the Chugach Range. How small we are at the base of such mountains.

Then comes the sound of the garage door closing. Everything disappears. There is just the two of us, and we are private people. I understand that when she holds her arm to me, a broken wing, it is an offering of compromised privacy. I smooth my hand over the calcified ridge. Some wounds heal. Her skin a pale scar under my fingertips, I want to tell her that if she had been my child, I would have protected her.

But what I say is, "My husband and I have two kids, a boy and a girl."

She nods once, then twice more. "I figured."

In the silence that follows, she opens the side door and peers out to the black night. "You got married young, didn't you?"

"I guess."

"That's good," she says, turning back to me. "Love is a good thing."

"It is." I'm thinking about my children. I try to focus solely on my feelings for him, my husband alone, but what comes to mind is how the kids look when they laugh, Jay still missing his two front teeth, Stella's bright eyes through her tangle of curls, and I know I can't separate him from them. "Love *is* a good thing." After a moment, I add, "I'm sorry."

"Why?"

"I just am."

She searches for her coat in the pile of down and wool and fleece as mine falls to the floor. I don't allow myself to think. One arm and then the next through the coat sleeves. When she walks out the door, so do I.

Stark autumn cold hits us and goes right to the marrow.

"It's always like this before the snow comes," I tell her as we walk to her car. "Freeze-up in Alaska is cruel."

Under our feet, the brown chaff of birch leaves. This year a big Chinook stripped trees to bones in a matter of hours, and then the cold stomped down on the yellow leaves, quickly grinding them to mash on the frozen ground.

"Not the beautiful season you're used to Outside, huh?" I say.

"Outside?"

"What we Alaskans call everywhere else."

She smiles, shakes her head.

"This is the Far North," I say. "Winter drops down hard on us. Like a hoof."

"When do you think it'll snow?"

"Soon, I hope. It's better when it does. Warmer. Brighter."

"I don't know if I'll ever get used to it here."

"It takes three winters." I remember I said those same words to my husband when I met him all those years ago. My father had just died of cancer, and it was my first year at UAF. I remember the lost feeling I'd carried within me, like a small skiff in big waves. So long ago, it's as though it happened to someone else, like I'm remembering someone else's life. Was that college freshman really me? Now a pulse of guilt beats through me. "If you make it three winters, you stay," I say. "You're Alaskan."

"Like you?"

"I was born here. I had no choice."

She stands back on her heels and regards me. "What's your deal?"

"What do you mean?"

She smiles, patient, and I see the scientist in her. White lab coat hunching over a microscope.

"I don't know that I have a deal."

The scientist waits.

I blow on my fingers.

"I can always tell," she says.

"Tell what?"

"About women. It's like identifying a mineral. You don't go by the color, you go by the fracture."

"What fracture? What are you talking about?"

"I'm talking about you."

I stare back at her. "What do you mean?"

"Suffering. That's what I mean."

I pull my coat tight around my neck. "But everybody suffers."

She nods, smiles at her data. "And?"

"And so what?"

In graduate school, she was mentored by her professor, favored above all the other students. When they talked about rocks, it was as though the two of them were in love with the same woman. But where there might have been jealousy, there was only passion. He sent her daily emails, and when they stopped to chat in the university's long echoing hallways, minutes ticked into hours. They were lost in events that occurred two billion years ago.

Once, late at night, she stopped by the lab to collect a forgotten scarf. Her professor was standing at the rows of rock specimen, his hands on the counter, and she could tell by his caved-in expression that he was not looking outward but inward to a different time.

She meant to leave quickly, to not disturb him, but he turned and said, "My wife had a strange habit. Whenever faculty would come for dinner, she would polish the baseboards and banisters, all the wood in the whole house. Always, that was that day she chose. I hated the smell of Murphy's Oil, and it would last throughout the dinner, overpowering whatever good smells were coming from the kitchen." He laid a hand on the counter, tapped a finger. "I see now that she did it simply for something to do. She was nervous having the university crowd over. She never felt worthy of the conversation." He laughed. "Rocks. Always about rocks."

Kris knew that his wife had been dead many years. "I'm sorry."

"And yet the parties were always her idea. I never would have thought of feeding people. She took care of me in that way, you know."

"You must have loved her a lot."

He smiled, turned back to the dusty rows. "I still do. Be careful with your tenses, my dear."

"I should go," she says, a glance to her car.

I take her hand in mine. It's cold as concrete. Another memory sparks, though this one is close to the moment, no question it is my life. "You know, you remind me of a woman I loved. A long time ago."

"Did she love you back?"

"No."

She smiles, tries to suppress it.

"Okay, so I was fourteen. She was my math teacher. She never knew."

Now she's laughing and soon I am too.

"I'm sure she did," Kris says. After a moment, she sobers and asks in a quiet voice, "Are you sorry the way things turned out?"

I look down at the frost on my thick rubber boots. I'm thinking about my children, how I sometimes wake in the night just to watch them sleep. "No."

The features of her face are a complex to me, a terrain of great depth and meaning. I want to remember her exactly as she is: eyes not blue but green in the moonlight, cheekbones sprinkled with last summer's freckles, a wide mouth with full, chapped lips. I tell myself that what I feel is an impulse, that's all.

But when she takes a step toward her car, a wild ticking starts up in me. Not an impulse but an instinct, like the instinct to keep warm.

Her hands are back in her pockets. "I should go." She draws in a breath, and when she releases it into the cold still night, the steam remains a cloud just above her head. "There is no institution that I respect more than marriage. Marriage and family," she says. "I've never experienced it, family I mean, but I've seen how it can be . . . in other people's lives. There's nothing more fundamental."

"That's true."

"And I'm not an asshole."

"Neither am I."

The cold presses in on us, heaving up from the leafy chaff under our feet and also dropping down from the stark bones of trees overhead. I reach for her, a hug good-bye, but there is the ticking within me now, too strong a pull, and I won't let go.

Her kiss is surprising. She is searching me with a particular purpose in mind, anticipating my reaction to her every movement. She is well trained. She kisses me deeply, pressing the small of my back, her hands so precise, a scientist's hands. I am discovered.

Her professor decided to take a trip to the Canadian Shield. He invited three students but cared only that she went. On the plane, they drank vodka tonics and discussed different qualities of granite and gneiss, giddy with anticipation of setting foot on Precambrian rock. He told her that there was amethyst between the Proterozoic and Archean layers, and she told him that she would like nothing more than to touch her fingers to it, even just for a moment. His eyes flashed under their shaggy brows, and he laid his age-freckled hand lightly over hers.

"Amethyst. My dear wife's birthstone."

She fell quiet.

He patted her knuckles and produced a baby blue handkerchief from between several pencils in his shirtfront pocket, wiped each wet eye and then his cracked lips. "And what can you tell me about amethyst?"

She was used to these drills. "Silicon dioxide," she said. "Six-sided prism ending in six-sided pyramid. Conchoidal fracture. Insoluble."

"Very good. But did you know that medieval soldiers wore it round their necks during battle?" He carefully folded the blue handkerchief and stowed it back between his pencils. "They believed the crystal would keep them safe in the cold world of war. Such was their faith in silicon dioxide."

And she understood that he was telling her something about love.

In her bed, our bodies shine white with moonlight. All I think about is right now. This moment. Her skin is unbearably soft over the workings of hard muscle and bone, and her small breasts press against mine. Deep in her hair, the scent of chlorine. She wears nothing but the charm strung around her neck on a loop of leather. Amethyst. And I wonder which is more beautiful. The crystal or its home at the hollow of the base of her throat?

She is more naked with her necklace than I am with nothing at all.

At the Canadian Shield, her professor, donned in a white Panama hat, kid leather gloves, and brand-new walking shoes, pulled his blue kerchief up over his mouth and nose. She told him he looked like a dapper terrorist, a description he rather liked. Soon the dust of the quartz pit stirred, and she had to hold her sleeve over her mouth.

They descended through the millennia, the layers bold and easy to read.

"Caldera," her professor sang out, pulling his kerchief from his face. "The Earth's most private and ancient recesses heaved up by volcanic explosion." He gave a grand stamp of his shellacked walking stick. After a moment, he added, "We're tourists, but I'm sorry to say that we are not, in fact, time travelers. We can read the drama that took place here, but that is all. We missed the action by billions of years."

The other students grew restless, dust-choked, and hungry. They shouldered their packs and climbed back to the present day. She and her professor stayed in the mine, no longer talking or taking samples or photographs, but simply remaining.

I displace the crystal and press my thumb in the hollow of her throat. A perfect fit. I look at the bedside clock and laugh. "I've known you for exactly eleven hours and thirty-six minutes."

"It doesn't matter how long."

Her words travel through my right hand. "True," I say. "It's just the beginning. The start."

Silence.

"What's wrong?"

She lifts my wrist and taps the gold band around my ring finger.

I fall back into her arms until morning. It's still dark and now I am crying. She refuses to negotiate. Frozen stiff, she's become a fountain statue, a piece of garden art. I continue to lie against her only because I don't know what else to do. I think, *I'll never say another word to you. Not even good-bye.* That will be her punishment.

I cast my gaze around her bedroom. The quarters of a bachelor: rented white walls, furnishings straight out of a box store display, a navy-blue bath towel slung across the bathroom door. There is nothing in the room that shows a private side of her, or any side at all. But then my eyes take in the crusted lump on her dresser. In the moonlight, the crystalline shades of color and intricacy are undecipherable, and her souvenir from the Miocene looks like nothing more than a chunk of concrete. My urge to hurt her falls away.

"In Iceland," I say, "they believe rocks have souls."

She stirs. She presses her face against mine, and I can feel that she's smiling.

I want to say something more to her, a compliment maybe, words of how beautiful she looks in the icy flood of moonlight. Or perhaps I want to tell her that I love my family and that she's torn my life apart. But I know that what she wants me to say is the one thing I can't: *You've had no effect on me at all.*

My thoughts turn to leaving as the sky goes light. I peer out the window and study the empty yard. The grass is green with just a trace of frost. I crack the window by an inch, and the air feels wet and cool against my skin. Then I see the dark, low clouds moving in.

"I know a little something about time, too. I can predict the future."

She looks at me with the solemnity of a child.

"Snow is coming."

"How do you know?"

I point to the gray mass plowing toward us.

"And it'll be warmer when it snows?"

I kiss her, and she kisses me back in that way of hers, and though I know that she won't last three years in Alaska or even three months, I release her and smile. Then I take her hand and hold it to the stream of air coming through the window.

PIKE

She heard that men have affairs like they have car accidents. They don't mean a thing by cheating; it just happens. For a woman, though, an affair is always a way out. Elizabeth couldn't remember where she heard this, a magazine, a friend—or when she heard it, before or after she was married. She knew it shouldn't matter. This sort of talk shows wisdom never meant a thing to her. And yet for the past two weeks, she's come back again and again to chase the possible significance of these words.

The fishing trip was her idea. She brought it up to her husband the night he reached a hand to her hip and, for the first time in their five-year marriage, she turned away. She could feel him breathing beside her, waiting for her to say something. Along the bedroom wall, car headlights flared and slid, one after the other, their light so brilliant she could sense it through closed lids. When she finally began to speak, it came in a rush. It came in a breathless rush that emanated from some dark place within her but must have seemed to him like a wonderful surprise: plans for a trip to his favorite trout fishing spot several hours from their Anchorage home.

He said the girls, Hannah and Zoe, would have fun hunting for tiny shrimp along the lakeshore, but Elizabeth said no. She'd rather it be just the two of them.

"So what's the occasion?" Bill asked. "This isn't like you."

"There is no occasion. We're just going fishing."

He looked at her and blinked, his lips curving into a half smile. "But you don't even like fishing."

She took up his big hand in hers and rubbed at the thick calluses there. His palms felt more like hard plastic than skin, toughened from so many years of building Montana log homes for the Anchorage elite. She worked her fingers in gentle circles, wondering if he could feel her touch.

"I haven't liked it *yet*," she said. "But I want to. I want to *learn* to like it."

The lake was three miles across, six miles wide, and over a hundred feet deep. Ringed by the greatest mountain ranges in Alaska—the Talkeetnas to the east, the Alaska to the north, the Chugach to the south, and the Wrangells to the west—the lake itself stood on a plateau two thousand feet above sea level. The day Elizabeth and Bill arrived, the lake reflected every bit of the turquoise sky above it. To Elizabeth's eyes, the water's shade was so striking it looked flame-like, hot to the touch. The chalky scent of warm bark and pine needles filled the air. It was as beautiful as he'd promised it would be.

This was her first visit, although he had been several times, staying free of charge in a friend's cabin. He tried his best to get her there a year ago, just after the miscarriage. Miscarriage. That was his word, and it was the doctor's word too because the baby was short of twenty weeks old, when the word stillborn would have applied.

If the baby had lived . . . but no, Elizabeth couldn't allow herself those fantasies. The baby hadn't lived. Instead, just before dawn on a night that Bill was on a job down in Kenai, Elizabeth had woken to great pain, and blood spilled from her. At the hospital, she delivered the dead baby at just nineteen weeks. A girl, her eyes were sealed shut in an expression of troubled sleep, and her hands, smaller than Elizabeth's fingertip, spread like tiny starfish. All was lost.

She did as best she could to move on. Still, she had refused the trip to Lake Louise last summer. She told Bill that the girls couldn't miss school—

Hannah had just started kindergarten and Zoe, preschool—plus there was all the work Elizabeth had yet to do, packing up the bright little room that they had filled far too early, certainly a curse. She told him if he wanted to go so bad, he'd just have to go alone. He argued that he didn't want to go so much as he thought it would do her some good to go, to help her get over the miscarriage.

She looked at him then as if he were a stranger sitting at her kitchen table. "And a fishing trip would accomplish that?" she asked. There was no anger in her voice. It was as if something in her had broken down, everything coming out flat and disconnected. "Fishing?"

Bill looked helplessly down into his plate of scrambled eggs. "You could try," he said, his voice cracking as though he might cry.

Now, one year later, she was there in the A-frame cabin overlooking the sparkling lake. Inside, there wasn't much furniture: an old brown corduroy couch, a shellacked stump for a coffee table, a stack of metal folding chairs leaning against a wall. In the corner beneath a bright green canopy of mosquito netting stood a king-sized bed, which her husband sat down on, bouncing slightly.

"Not much to look at," he said. "But it'll do. Want to take it for a test drive?"

"So is it true," Elizabeth said quickly, turning away from him and pointing out the window to the lake below, "that we're in a trout fisherman's paradise? Lakers the size of salmon?"

Her husband stood and stretched. "Used to be true. Let's hope that's still the case."

"They've been fished out?"

"Not fished out. Slaughtered."

"Slaughtered? By who?"

"By other fish. Goddamned northern pike. They're not native, but some idiot stocked the lake years ago, and now the pike are killing all my fish. It's happening all over the state. Wolf fish is what they are. Aggressive little bastards, nothing but teeth and attitude. And ugly as sin. The big ones get so long and flat they almost look like crocodiles." He shook his head. "The day's coming when there won't be a single beautiful trout left in this lake."

While her husband went to see about renting a skiff, she stood on the small deck overlooking the lake and watched the sun sparkle off the water. She couldn't make out the far shore but rising beyond that, what she initially mistook for clouds, was the ghostly outline of what must be Mount Sanford, the highest peak of the Wrangell Mountain Range. She breathed in the unseasonably warm, dry air. And then she closed her eyes, pushed her fingers against them, and thought: For a woman, an affair is always a way out. As intentional as a slit wrist.

A way out? She wasn't sure. But she knew this much, what she had done wasn't a way into something else. He was just a boy, really, barely past his teens. Sparse golden stubble and a chest so hairless and pale and flat it must have been an embarrassment to him. He wore his hair long, the filthy laces of his Chuck Taylor's went untied, and a ridiculous necklace of orange plastic beads hung from his neck. There'd been only the one time. She hadn't wanted another.

How could she explain it? There had been weeks of rain. Weeks and weeks of rain, housebound with the girls. Such gray weeks that she lost her ability to see past them. And then one day out came the sun. It cracked from the clouds—cracked like an egg—the bright yolk slipping out and stunning the wet little town, bathing everything in a most golden light.

This, of course, explained nothing. This was a weather report.

When her husband returned with the skiff, she apologized and told him she was exhausted, that he'd have to go it alone for the afternoon.

"So I'm on my own to catch dinner?" he said, trying for a jovial tone, but his big shoulders drooped and his arms hung at his sides. He looked at her then, and as he looked, he turned his head slightly, bit at his lip rather than say anything more. After a moment, he turned and walked heavily down the wooden stairs that led to the dock.

It hadn't been just the boy who caught her attention. A group of them were playing Frisbee, boys and girls, filled with such a wild, horse-like energy, as though they'd just piled from the gloomy dorm into that burst of sunshine. Elizabeth had been struck by the scene, by the simple joy of it all. Though she had groceries, some of them melting in the back of her Subaru, she sat down on a park bench, took off her shoes, and stretched an arm along the warm painted wood. Only then did she see him apart from the others. She studied his movements. No, she memorized them. Shirtless and leaping through the golden air, his hair throwing off sparks of light as he caught and spun the disk—it was an effortless choreography. Every age has its grace, but for this boy, this fragile-chested boy, no amount of wisdom or confidence or experience would ever compare to what he had right at that moment playing Frisbee with such abandon.

More weather report. The sky cracked open and there he was.

A boat motor droned and grew louder with each breath she drew. When she heard the motor cut, she parted the dark curtain of mosquito netting, swung her legs down from the bed, and sat clutching the mattress. She felt a stabbing loneliness for her children.

"Goddamned pike!" Bill yelled. He was a big man, his frame filled the doorway, and she couldn't help but startle at the sound of his voice. "These hillbillies think anything goes," he said. "What's one more fish in the lake. The more the merrier." He shook his head. "They think nature can handle anything. But you know, ecosystems are incredibly delicate. It doesn't take much to throw everything out of balance." He sat beside her on the bed, wrapping his arms around her. "They've beaten us," he said. "We're stuck with chicken for dinner."

She prepared wild rice on the propane stove, then salted and wrapped the chicken breasts in tinfoil along with sliced red potatoes and sprigs of rosemary. Her husband loved rosemary. At home, she grew it in tiny cups on the windowsill, feeding it water by the teaspoon, turning it daily toward the light.

"Not bad," Bill said, tearing apart the wing, "even if it is chicken."

After dinner, they sat drinking Bailey's and hot chocolate on the porch, listening to a loon howling away for his mate.

Her husband moved a hand to Elizabeth's knee. The August Alaskan sky had gone from deep gray to black, and she knew it must be quite late. Pumping the lantern, she stood up in order to strike a match and was relieved when his hand fell away. But as soon as she sat down again, she felt his touch. Her eyes adjusted to the flickering light and she studied his hand. She could just make out the network of scars across his knuckles, remnant of a years' ago building accident. It occurred to her she'd only seen Bill cry once, when she lay naked and quiet on the crisp white paper of the examining table. He laid his big scarred hand spread across her belly and wept like a little boy. Nothing came from her, no tears or words, she just studied the crushed skin of his knuckles and thought again and again: *Yesterday was Monday, so today is Tuesday. Garbage day. Today is garbage day.*

"At least the loons are still here," he said now, startling her.

She smiled faintly, a loneliness for her children rising again within her, stabbing at her.

"How about we go in now?" he said. "I'll let you ravage me."

"But it's so nice out here. You know what I'd like to do is go down to the dock for a while."

It was a small dock, room for just the two of them side by side. Three strides and they had reached the end. The planks were weathered gray and felt smooth and cool under her bare feet. "I can't get enough of this air," he said, inhaling deeply. "It may be an Alaskan Indian summer, so warm for August, but there's no mistaking that smell. The night air brings it out. You just know freeze-up is coming."

The loon called again and though it sounded quite close, it was too dark to spot. Her husband wrapped an arm around her waist, completely encircling her. She used to love the possessiveness of his touch. The first time he held her, not long after they met, it came as a shock, how natural the touch of a near stranger had felt.

Now, in his arms, she could only think this: Men have affairs like accidents; women have affairs to slit their wrists.

Something splashed quite close in the darkness. They both turned toward it. She took a step forward, lining her toes with the very ends of the boards. Below her nothing but black water.

He swept up her hair and began to kiss the back of her neck.

"Hold on," she said, breaking away. "What is it out there? A loon? Can you make it out?"

"It's all our beautiful trout. Tomorrow they'll be jumping right into our boat." He started kissing her again.

"Bill, wait," she said.

"Oh, come on. I mean, have I done something?"

She shook her head quickly. "No, no, you haven't done anything. I'm just—" she leaned against him. "Nothing. There's just so much going on out there."

They listened, but whatever had been splashing in the dark water was silent now.

"Well, then, I hate to tell you this," he said, moving in to hold her again, "but we're in Alaska and in this state, it's actually illegal for a wife to refuse her husband."

Though he couldn't see her face, she forced a smile. "Is that a fact?"

"I'm dead serious. And they don't just fine you. You could actually get years in the pen for this offense."

"A jail sentence? That sounds pretty severe." The loon howled again. Her throat had gone dry. "So you're going to call the rangers on me?"

"No," he said, turning her around. "I don't believe I'll need any assistance from the rangers."

She looked up at him then and felt as though the night was pressing in on her, forcing the air from her lungs. But she took her husband's hand firmly in her own and led him back up to the cabin. She thought any sort of pleasure would be impossible for her now. She'd forgotten how well he knew her; that he understood just how to move within her. She came not once but twice.

After, she lay awake hungry for the feel of her children against her skin. As babies, they used to sleep pressed against her breasts, Bill's arms around them all. Now she felt a longing for them, and for him, for the part of him that surrounded them. A longing like grief.

The lake had been dead calm in the early morning, but by ten o'clock, as they sped to a suspected hole on the far shore, the waves had picked up. Her husband nodded toward the treed horizon. "See that?" he said. A jumble of distant clouds shed a grainy haze that stretched into the tree line. There was no sign of Mount Sanford or any of the mountain ranges ringing the lake. "Rain," he said. "We probably only have an hour or so at best. Feel lucky?"

He dropped a switch and the boat slowed to a troll. "First thing," he said, "if you want to catch a monster, you gotta use a monster lure." He pulled a silver and blue metal fish from his tackle box. Three sets of dangerous-looking hooks glinted from the head, belly, and tail; its painted eyes held the same stunned expression as a real fish. As she took it carefully from his hand, the barbs hanging from the dorsal fin swung and caught on her sleeve.

He crouched beside her and as she watched his big fingers work delicately with the lure, a pressure rose up in her throat. She knew those hands so well. With those hands he made his living, he fed her children, he made love to her. If he had a soul, she knew it resided there.

"Okay, you're set," he said. "Just put the rod in the holder and you're fishing." He tied a similar lure to his pole and moved to the opposite side of the boat. "Just keep an eye on that tip. It's bobbing now from the weight of the lure, but if you see it really start to bend, grab it and give it a good yank to set the hook."

He leaned back in the driver's chair and sighed.

"So all we do is wait?" she asked.

"It's the easy life for us. Having fun yet?"

She kept her eyes on the rod tip, its dipping rhythm hypnotizing.

"HOLY SHIT!" her husband yelled, startling her. "FISH ON!" He grabbed for the rod. The boat rocked so violently that she had to cling to the sides. The rod bent nearly double. The whizzing of his reel sounded across the quiet lake. He gave it a turn and shook his head. "I should have put heavier line on! What was I thinking?"

She looked into the water but saw not even a ripple. The fish had taken the line way out. "A big one?"

"If I can land it," he said, "it'll be the biggest trout I ever caught."

She hated herself for asking the question, but couldn't stop: "How are you so sure it's a trout?"

"Too much fight in it to be a pike. Reeling those bastards in is like pulling up a log—just dead weight." He strained against the pole, bending it double. "What I have here," he said, the words pressing out from between clenched teeth, "is a glory fish."

Then he looked over at her, broke into a smile. "Correction," he said. "What *you* have here." He dragged the rod over to her.

"What? No, Bill. I don't even know what I'm doing. I'll lose it."

"So? That's the name of the game, darling. Fishing is all about heartbreak." He jutted his chin toward the rod.

She took it, and the rod immediately jumped to life in her hands. All she could do was hold on; the drag of the line gave her a taste of the power in that fish.

"Just let it run for a while," he said. "That's one fish that wants to be free. It'll turn soon."

But the fish wasn't turning. The line was running out. Her husband flipped the boat in reverse, hoping to chase it down. It was too late, though, the line was nearly gone.

"Fucking hell," he said. "I'm going to have to adjust the tension. It'll probably snap." She gave him the rod and waited for the line to break.

It didn't. It bent nearly double, the line whizzing, and then it sprang back out and everything went silent.

"It turned!" he yelled. "Start reeling! Reel like crazy!"

She cranked for all she was worth. It started to fight then and for a minute she could barely turn the handle. "What on earth is it, Bill? This can't be a fish!"

"It's a big fucking whale is what it is! They'll name the lake after you."

She pulled back, putting her whole body in motion against the fish. Her heart beat wildly in her chest. She wanted to do this. She wanted to land this fish. It was a sharp, clean feeling. An honest feeling. One that filled her with hope. "I can do this!" she said.

"Keep reeling. It's burning out."

She pulled back as hard as she could.

"I see it!" he said, pointing.

"Where? Where?"

"There! It just rolled way under the surface. You're close!"

She reeled. Though her thumb was raw and fingers stiff with pain, she reeled. Then she saw it. A dark form gliding stealthily up, rolling, then disappearing back into the bright turquoise water. A terrible feeling shook her, as if her organs had been clapped together. In that instant, she changed her mind. She no longer wanted to bring this creature into the boat.

"Here it is!" Bill yelled. The water's surface exploded. He leaned far out of the boat with a large, fluorescent green net and swung it into the center of the spray. Straining, he hoisted it into the boat and dropped it on the floor. It was very big. The body long and flat as an eel, the spacing of the pectoral fins giving it that crocodile-look. It had a long, snubbed nose that took up most of its head and a terrible jaw, which was thrust out in a defiant underbite, showing off a mouth filled with tiny, pointed teeth.

"Well," her husband said, lifting the net away, "I'd guess it's over twenty pounds." He smiled at her, trying to keep the disappointment from his eyes. "Now that's a big fish where I come from."

Elizabeth watched as it flopped violently at her feet, its mouth gaping wide. Her husband dropped the net back over the fish and then set his boot down on it. "But you know what this is, right?"

She turned her back to him. Yes, she recognized this fish. She wrapped her arms tightly around herself and said, "Bill." She said it quietly, but in a way that made him turn to her. She stood for a moment listening to the small waves lap at the aluminum boat, unable to return his gaze, nor could she keep staring down at the terrible fish. She squinted out across the lake.

He laughed. He said, "What?" Then he said, "Come on. It's okay. Don't take it so hard."

She stayed quiet, watching the dark mass of clouds closing in on them.

"What?" he said again, his voice different now, pitched lower.

She imagined telling him about the weeks of rain and about how the sun that day had cracked like an egg from the clouds, and she imagined telling him about the boy, how it seemed that the boy, too, had slipped out from the just-opened sky. But none of it, she knew, would mean a thing to him. All he would understand is that she had just slit open the vein of their family.

"What?" he said again, quieter, touching her arm.

Her knees swayed with a sharp violence as she fell against him in an embrace. She held him tight, her arms reaching up around his neck. "I love you," she said. There was panic in her throat and it filled her words. She'd never felt so far from him and thought he must sense it. But when she let him go, sitting heavily down in the turned-out driver's seat, his face broke into an open smile. He reached out to touch her with his damaged hand.

"I love you too," he said.

He sat opposite her on the plank bench and lifted the net away from the pike. He stepped gently on its side. They both looked down at the fish between them. It was no longer thrashing but arching its long, muscular body in great slow curls against his boot, its gills gasping open and closed more slowly now, its spike-toothed mouth gaping soundlessly at the air that was killing it.

LONG WEEKEND

My house in Anchorage had become a monument to all that X took away.
There, under the big picture window, an empty space where the red leather
couch used to be, the one that matched the loveseat, which was also gone.
The potted fig tree that once stood next to the missing loveseat, taken, so too
the towering bookshelf across the room, which was just as well since there
were no books to be shelved, not anymore. We hadn't been married long.
Most of our pre-wedding wealth was in the currency of gear: avalanche bea-
cons, ice axes, forty-below bags, etc. Only recently had we come to justify
spending money on items that wouldn't save our lives, but there had been
quite a bit of wedding loot, plus the big-ticket splurge of new furniture on
our first anniversary. I let him have it all, and now my mother was coming
to visit.

Although she had named me after herself, Barbara, we couldn't be more
different. When I told her about the divorce, she first begged me to forgive
him the barista affair, and when I explained we simply didn't love each other

anymore, she said, "Love Shmov!" It took her several phone calls to finally accept that X and I were parting and then several more to give up on the annulment idea. I remember wailing into the phone like a teenager, "Who gets annulments anymore, Ma? Nobody, that's who!" But when I laid out the terms of the divorce for her, explaining that at least I was able to buy X out of his half of the house plus keep Easy, our elderly diarrhea-prone Bernese mix, she croaked back, *Put up your dukes and fight the bastard!*

In the half hour before her plane landed, I surveyed my small living room and ran my hands through Easy's soft coat. I was left with what X didn't want: the wine-stained woven rug from my post-college trip to Morocco, a secondhand white Formica dining table with two mismatched wooden chairs, a piece of plywood on several milk crates that served as our coffee table. But some of the things he took couldn't have been worth much, like our music collection. Most of the well-worn records had been mine—some of them birthday presents from my dad, who died when I was still a teen. An eclectic blend of the Stones and Michael Jackson, Devo and Ella Fitzgerald, Joni Mitchell and Duran Duran. There were also old 45s and a couple of 78s, a stack of eight-tracks, plus cases of cassettes, even a box of mix tapes from the various loves of my life. Of all that he took, the music is what I grieved.

I ran the vacuum one more time and wiped down the plywood coffee table, lodging a splinter into my palm. I found a safety pin and wasted precious time looking for the rubbing alcohol, which was missing from the medicine cabinet along with Band-Aids and ibuprofen. There was whiskey, though, because I bought it on the day the divorce was finalized. I splashed Tullamore on my palm and the pin, took a long swallow, and then dug the splinter out.

On the way to the airport, the late summer rain froze. Noise like a thousand hooves trampling my roof and I couldn't see a thing. I glanced at Easy in the rearview mirror. Unconcerned, he faced straight ahead, gazing at the gray nothingness ahead of us. I pulled over to the side of the road to wait it out. Rolling down the window a bit, I stretched out my open hand. I missed several hailstones as they pelted my skin and bounced off, but then I caught one. Big and jagged, what had felt so solid as they hit were actually several distinct ice crystals, lacy wings entwined, clinging together, and for just a moment, I found it unfathomable that such delicate beauty as this had fallen freely from the sky. Then the outer lace disappeared into tiny beads of liquid, and soon my palm was damp and empty.

It occurred to me that my mother's plane would be unable to land in the storm. I imagined the aircraft angling back to Chicago (or Seattle, or Portland, or *wherever*). But no. My phone buzzed in the console.

"Where are you?" she said in greeting. "I've already got my bags."

"Pinned down by weather. Maybe you haven't noticed, Ma, but the world is ending."

"Well," she said, "my pilot managed to land a 737 just fine."

She hadn't visited Alaska in over five years, since my wedding, which she insisted on calling my celebration because it didn't take place in a Catholic church. It was safer to see her on her own turf, Chicago, where I was not expected to take charge or entertain or do much of anything at all. I could hide under the covers in my childhood bedroom and stare at my older sister's wall of faded spelling bee ribbons. Second place, third place, forever enshrined by my mother's fierce pride.

"I'll be there as soon as I can see the road," I said and hung up.

At the airport I hesitated as my mother wheeled her suitcase through the double-glass doors. She looked old. Thin to the point of frail, her eyes full of defeat, and though she was wearing a designer suit, she had the air of a refugee. Palestine, Croatia, Vietnam, in all the pictures I had ever seen, the old women carry the same look: I've worked hard my whole life and now this shit?

"Ma!" I leapt from the car and waved.

"Airplane travel," she called back indignantly, pausing to catch her breath, "has certainly changed over the years." She cast a menacing look at the innocents passing by. "Anyone flies now. Just like taking the city bus! Nobody dresses for it, either. Not anymore they don't."

You would think her last flight was 1958. She flew all the time—New York, Paris, even Morocco a couple of years ago. She traveled with a group of hard-drinking senior citizens, which she suffered for the enjoyment of complaining about them.

I reached out to hug her, but she wrapped her hand around my arms and gripped tight, keeping me at a distance. "I had a bit of an accident last spring. I'm still healing, so just a smile will do, thank you."

"An accident? Like a car accident?"

"No, I was just being clumsy."

"What? What do you mean? Did you fall?"

"A misstep is all."

"Did you break something?"

"Just my back."

"Your back? You broke your back? Why didn't you call me?"

She moved to the car and pulled open the passenger door. "A lot of people break their backs, Barbara. Some break their backs and don't even know it."

"This is crazy, Ma. Do Mary and Pete know?" Mary and Pete were my older siblings, Irish twins born ten months apart. "Tell me you at least called Mary."

She winced as she eased herself into the car. "I didn't want to bother her. Mary is busy enough as it is."

Easy leaned forward to sniff my mother's ear. She giggled like a coy girl and lay a hand on his snout. "And how is His Handsomeness?"

"Arthritic."

She shut her eyes and placed her cheek against his jowls. "We're getting old, you and me. People are beginning to notice."

As I started the car, my sense of guilt edged to anger. "Next time you break your back, at least give me a call, okay?"

"Oh, what are you going to do about it all the way in Alaska?"

"Only a few hours by plane, Ma."

"It's the ends of the earth." She pulled down the mirror and began to arrange her silver hair. "Do you have some nice wine in the house?"

"I do."

She cast a suspicious eye over me. "What kind?"

"Both. Red and white."

She put a finger to her forehead. "Easy, please explain to your mother that red and white are simply colors." She brushed at her navy suit pants. "A nice Pinot Grigio would be wonderful, but no. I'm sure whatever you have is fine."

My mother was a fluent speaker of opposites. I drove into Spenard and stopped at In and Out Liquors, insisting she wait in the car. Of course she followed me, and we were anything but "in and out." She finally settled on a Pinot Grigio. which, when we arrived home, I poured into a jelly jar for her. Not long ago I owned a set of eight short-stem wine glasses, but they went the way of X.

"Well," my mother said, peering around the room over her jar of wine. She was having a difficult time finding a proper hold on it. She unhappily clasped her two small hands around the jar, as though it were a hot mug of coffee. "This is much nicer than your last apartment. A whole house to yourself! Just think it!"

I waited for her to start right in on the divorce. But she said, "I never had a house of my own. Never, I mean, until Mary got married and left home. First, there were my parents and all of my brothers, six of them, if you can imagine. Then there was your father."

"You could have, you know."

"What?"

"You could have had the house to yourself much sooner by putting Mary out. What was she, thirty? Pete and I were gone at eighteen."

"Oh," she said, waving her jar of wine, "to tell the truth, I don't like living alone. It's not natural. People were meant to live in groups. Family groups. Not alone."

She missed ruling over other people. "Suits me just fine."

She leaned in and placed a hand on my knee. "You think you do, but just wait. Drifting around without a family at the ends of the earth, without anyone who cares about you, no husband."

"Ma! You said you wouldn't."

"Of course I don't just mean you singular, dear. I mean your entire generation. Just out for yourselves, moving here and there, across the world from your home, your people." She turned to Easy and whispered, "Soft and spoiled, all of them. And divorced."

"I specifically laid out the terms of your visit, and you promised—"

"Your generation, sweetheart. Now I read that today's young people aren't even getting married anymore. No longer fashionable." She took a slow sip of her wine, offering me a sly look over the glass rim. "I give you credit. At least you gave it a try."

I stood up, though where could I go? She was here in my house, where she would remain for days. There was no escape. "I better put the bottle in the fridge."

In the kitchen, I rested my forehead against the cool plastic of the refrigerator. There was no explaining my life to my mother. It had always been that way. How could she ever understand the way things had turned between X and me. Somewhere in all of our years together, we had lost our connection. We were no longer interested in the same things. Conversations became an exercise in patience. All he ever wanted to talk about was climbing. And he bragged. Going on about all the peaks he had bagged: the unnamed ones, the unclimbed ones, how many times he had been weathered in or injured, telling the same damn stories when he was drunk. How could I explain to my mother that, toward the end, I didn't even like X anymore? I couldn't stand to be around him.

Three days, I told myself, and then she would be gone.

When I came back into the living room, my mother straightened with a spry look, though I could see past it to the exhaustion in her eyes. Her shoulders, too, rounded and drooped despite her battle for posture.

"That's a lovely little rug," she said.

"Thank you." I waited for her to mention the stain, but she just smiled at me. I was getting a funny feeling. "What?" I finally said.

"Okay, I do have a matter I would like to discuss with you," she started, flirtatious as a schoolgirl, "but it can wait until dinner. I don't presume you've prepared anything? Shall we go out?"

We drove downtown, catching the late summer sun low over the water. She asked me to pull over to watch for a minute. High tide hid the mudflats, and the gray waters of Cook Inlet sparkled in the late sunlight. Far in the distance floated the mirage-like white shoulders of our highest peak, Denali. The mountain, along with nearby Hunter and Foraker, shone against a pale sky. X had climbed them all, talking about them as though he owned them. Still, I wondered what it felt like to stand at the very top, so far from the world below. Maybe there was no coming back from the experience.

My mother was uncharacteristically quiet. I was relieved, though soon grew uncomfortable. She was lost in some reverie, her face falling into sadness. I wanted to ask her what she was thinking about, but something held me back. A habit of protecting my privacy by ignoring her.

After some time, she laid her thin hand on my arm and whispered, "Thank you."

The restaurant was upscale, but she studied the other patrons with a frown.

"Blue jeans?" she whispered.

"It's Alaska. They show up at formal occasions in their Levi's, too."

"Oh, yes. How could I forget your wedding?"

I lifted the oversize menu as a barrier between us. For years, her favorite topic of conversation was my wedding guests in jeans. She even wrote a postcard to her childhood friend about it.

When the server—a white girl in dreadlocks—arrived, my mother eyed her and sniffed, then split the menu open with a theatric crack. As soon as the young woman was out of earshot, my mother said, "Why do they do it? Pretty girls doing everything to ruin their looks."

"It's called style, Ma."

"That's not the word I would use. Do you remember when you shaved your head. Good Lord. When I was young, we spent time and effort making ourselves look pretty, not like concentration camp survivors. And you did it right before prom, as I remember."

"So, what looks good on the menu?"

"I used to spend hours doing my hair before a date." She sighed. "I remember the first date I had with your father. Humphrey Bogart in *The Harder They Fall*. It was 1956, and I was seventeen years old."

"Really?" I looked up from the menu. My father was the one subject I actually liked hearing her talk about. "So how did the date go?"

"So-so," she said.

"So-so?"

"We weren't engaged yet, and I was dating two or three other fellas."

"Two or three?" I laughed. "I hope you left some for the other girls!"

"Things were different then. We played the field. But we weren't hopping into the sack left and right either."

"And how would you know what people today are doing?" I asked, smiling.

"I read. I know what's going on in the world." She took a sip of water. "Your father made a big show of buying me anything I wanted at the concession stand—popcorn, soda pop, candy—and I kept pointing through the glass counter for more. I was testing him, you see. And I liked him well enough." She was silent for a moment, tapping a bony white finger against the burgundy tablecloth. The look on her face was difficult to read; the same that always took hold when she studied For Sale by Owner ads in the newspaper, which she had done religiously every morning for as long as I can remember. She leaned back in her chair and said, as if to no one in particular, "I remember thinking, well, Barb, he's no great shakes, he's no Humphrey Bogart, but a girl could do worse. We were married that same year."

"A girl could do worse?" I said, loud enough for the people next to us to glance our way. My mother was pragmatic through and through. I remember as a child, she used to put the three of us in the tub all together, scrubbing and dousing and drying us with all the feeling of a factory worker. A girl could do worse! These were the words that she built her life around? "It must have been some romance."

"That's what movies are for, dear. Real life is about real people. It's about taking care of each other." Now she paused. For a long moment she remained quiet, a look of dismay sweeping across her features. "Listen to me, honey. Please. Just listen to me." She took up my hand in both of hers. "I'm worried."

The server returned with our drinks and asked for our order. I was grateful for the interruption and pulled my hands away. I didn't want to hear what she had to say. Whatever it was, I knew I couldn't bear it.

I ordered the halibut cheeks and forced levity into my voice as the waitress left us. "Humphrey Bogart. I don't know, Ma. I guess I never quite got him. I mean, he wasn't even attractive with that hangdog face. Now Cary Grant, I understand."

She waved off my comment, then made a grab for my hand. "Come home, darling."

"What?"

"Come back to Des Plaines."

I blinked at her.

"I was thinking to myself, Mary is fine now. She's got Steve, thank the heavens, and seems to have finally found her way. And you know Peter, he's always been fine. But you, I worry about you."

I leaned back in my chair and stared at the ceiling. Three days, I thought. Two really.

"You're not getting any younger, my dear."

"Thank you for reminding me."

"And here you are, all alone in the cold. All alone at the ends of the earth."

"Don't you think you're being a bit dramatic?"

"And so I've decided to give you the house. You were born there. It's rightfully yours. I know your dear father would agree. He loved that little house so. And the two of us can live there until I die, then it will be yours alone."

I laughed, long and hard, and then I took a swallow of wine. "Ma." How could I phrase this? I lifted the glass to my lips once more. "Okay, so here's the thing. You don't even like me. And quite honestly, I don't like you. Let's face it, we can't stand one another."

Her pleading look turned quizzical. "Well, what does that have to do with the price of tea in China?"

I shook my head in disbelief.

"The house will be in your name."

"No. No thank you. Thank you, but no."

"All I am asking is that you please think about it."

"Not even if hell freezes over. How's that for a thought?"

She lifted my hand in hers again, such a firm grasp, like the talons of an eagle. Her eyes shone bright blue under asymmetrical penciled brows—she was either losing her touch or her eyesight. Her suit jacket a size or two too large, I was struck again by just how much her body had withered. But those eyes still burned, and in fact appeared bigger and bolder than ever before. Shrinking flesh and bone revealed more of the spirit pulsing underneath. "Think it over."

The next morning I awoke to the sound of talking from the kitchen, my mother's voice. For one wild moment, I thought X had come back. But no, it was just my mother prattling on to Easy. His bloodshot, sagging, bored-out-of-his-mind eyes brought some consolation to me.

"I hope I didn't wake you," she said. "Easy and I were just in the middle of a heart-to-heart."

I leaned against the kitchen doorframe, eying the coffeepot and then noticing that my mother was wearing an apron. Where did it come from? Did she *pack* it?

"I was thinking," she said, "how about we take a drive today? You can show me the sights. We can picnic on the beach."

"Ma, I don't think you'd like the beach in Alaska, especially today. It looks windy out."

"I want to see what Captain Cook saw before they ate him."

"That was the Hawaiians."

"Regardless, I would like to see where he sailed."

"Well, I don't think it's going to be the sort of beach you think it'll be."

"As long as there's water."

We picked up sandwiches from the deli, including a pastrami and Swiss for Easy, and drove down to Beluga Point. An outcrop of rock between the highway and the ocean, I hadn't stopped here for years, preferring more remote locations. There was a cold, steady breeze, and I had to help her as we picked our way farther out. We found a somewhat sheltered spot and sat down. Easy grunted as he lowered himself beside my mother.

"Poor old thing," my mother said, petting his head. "Getting old is not fun, is it?"

"He's not that old. Ten is like middle age for a dog."

She shook her head. "For a big dog like this, no dear. Ten is advanced old age. He'll be lucky to live another year."

"Thanks, Ma. Cheerful."

She hunted through the sandwiches, unwrapped the pastrami, and held it to Easy's long snout. "Just telling you how it is."

The waves were up, and in the distance, I could see Gull Rock on the point miles past the tiny town of Hope. Years ago, X and I had hiked from the town to the point. The trip took hours, though it was an easy hike, mostly flat. I didn't remember what we talked about that day, or if we had much conversation at all, but I did recall the rhythm of walking with him down the trail. I felt so close to him by the time we reached Gull Rock, just the two of us surrounded by all that water.

I nudged my mother and pointed across the arm. "That's Hope over there."

"We went there after your wedding, remember? Nice name for a town. Hope."

The sun shone, setting off the distant snow on the Alaska Range. What had happened to those two newlyweds, X and me? How did we ever come to decide to part ways? It seems odd now. I thought of all the lazy Sundays when we would sleep late, make love, and spend hours reading the *New York Times* over coffee. And every night I used to wake to feel his warm presence in bed with me.

I studied the brilliant white peaks, sharp against the immense blue sky. X could be up there right now, for all I knew. He could be anywhere.

"Have you thought over our little conversation, Barbara?"

"What?"

"From last night."

"Ma, please."

"I thought you might have . . . reflected a bit on where you fit into the scheme of things. Up here all alone."

"I guess you haven't noticed all of the other people who live in Alaska."

"But honey, you know what I mean. You have no family here."

I was angry, but my reaction felt less like an emotion than a muscle flexing against her. A muscle I had spent my young life developing against her, powerful enough to make me slam doors and weep into my pillow or stay out all night smoking pot at friends' houses. "Ma, you have to get it into your head that I'm not coming home. Ever."

But even as I was yelling the word, another thought hit me: Where was my home? X was gone from my life, and he would never come back. Tears burned my eyes, but I fought them.

"Anyway, what does it matter?" My mother said, her voice breaking. "Who cares what an old lady wishes for? Who cares what anyone wishes? Wishing ain't getting, is it?"

"I'm not falling for your crap, Ma."

She glared at me, opening her mouth for a fight. But just as quickly, she turned away from me toward the inlet.

Soon her shoulders began to shake slightly. At first, I thought she was laughing, but no. She was crying. My mother was crying. I had never once in my entire life seen her cry. Like a small child, I was inflated with my own sense of wrongdoing.

I put my arm around her. She heaved against me.

Patting her as I would an infant, I felt the fragile bones of her back through her jacket. *Stop crying*, I thought. *Please just stop*. We were out on a dangerous precipice, and all I wanted was to inch back to safety.

"Enough," my mother finally said. She wiped her cheek with the back of a glove and shook her head. "Listen to me carry on like this." She took out a scarf and wrapped it tightly around her hair. "Old fool."

Relief swept through me. She was my mother once again.

A cold draft swept over the water, and she steeled herself against it, clasping the topmost button of her jacket. "After all, life isn't for sissies, is it?"

My mother insisted on taking the train to the airport. The train station was farther and less convenient for me than the airport, but she said she wanted the experience. She had her heart set on looking out the window at me while we waved good-bye. I groaned in exasperation but agreed.

We waited on the platform with a small crowd of strangers as a dark mass of clouds gathered across the water. I wondered if the rain would make its way to us. Sometimes weeks went by with rain in the mountains to the east, while my part of town remained dry. But out at sea, there was nothing to hold the rain clouds.

My mother gave me a dramatic but gentle hug before turning to the old bearded porter, holding her hand out to him until he got the idea and helped her onto the train.

I had Easy on a leash, and when I tried to walk along to find my mother at her window, it took him several attempts to stand.

"Come on, boy. You can do it." His sagging lower lids made his eyes appear remorseful. I patted him. "It's okay. We don't have to walk. We'll just stay here and watch her go past."

There were only seven or eight people left on the platform. As the whistle blew and the train began to chug along, I caught sight of my mother's bright silver hair in the window of the third car. She rapped on the glass, a tiny old woman, her face a mask of wrinkles, and the train lurched past. She was gone.

A tightness clamped down on my chest. I couldn't breathe. *This could very well be it*. I dropped Easy's leash and began to jog alongside the train. *The very last time*. And then I was running, pumping my legs for all I was worth. "Wait!" I screamed. "I'm sorry! Don't leave me!"

I waved high above my head as the train pulled away. But just then, I saw her hand, my mother's thin hand, extend from an open window.

"Good for you," somebody yelled. I turned to see a woman with a stroller smiling and nodding. Then a man with a mustache shouted, "Don't give up on him, honey!"

Soon all along the platform, strangers were clapping. They carried on as though this were some sort of romantic Hollywood ending, the kind my mother had always wanted.

PAINKILLERS

I lie in the soft wet lawn of the house I just cleaned, high on the expired cherry cough syrup I scored this afternoon from my client's bathroom vanity. I also made off with a vial of last year's Valium. In this rich Anchorage neighborhood, somebody might call the cops on a guy like me passed out in their yard, but it's another hour until the bus comes, and there's no bench or shelter. I wish Anna were lying here with me. The housecleaning business was her idea, but lately I'm the one doing all the work.

She's setting up her show in the warehouse by now. Her mentor arranged it all, and he's probably there with her at this very moment. I've never met him, but judging by the way Anna talks about him (or strategically *doesn't* talk about him), I don't like him. I keep coming across his business cards around the apartment, which I discreetly shred or crumple, depending on my mood. Once I found one of his cards stuck in the book I was reading. How did it get there? I must have grabbed it from the bedside table. If so, how did it get to the table on *my* side of the bed?

Bad enough the guy has a card, but it's such a pretentious card. All white, with a bold black font like from an old-fashioned typewriter: *Rodolfo Luis Jimenez Anaya*. And the only other information is his social media, like he's too important to have to explain who he is or give out his number. Please. And are four names really necessary? Four? I manage to get by just fine, and I don't even have a middle name.

I tug at the busted zipper on my leather jacket—no dice—and then cross my arms over my chest. The syrup is keeping me warm enough in the late August chill. So, what if he *is* there with her right now? Has he been breaking his back every day to keep her in Grape Nuts and peanut butter? Did he go to college with her? I know Anna's whole family and that is a hell of a lot of people. They're Filipino, well, Filipino American, and they are the kind of family that are always celebrating someone or something. Birthdays, graduations, weddings, funerals. They cook for days and have to rent banquet rooms to fit everybody. And they all love me: her cousins, her aunts and uncles, her grandmother, even her grandmother's neighbor. When you have an in with your girlfriend's grandmother's neighbor, you're solid, right?

Rodolfo Luis Jimenez Anaya. Is that a Filipino name? Could he be Filipino? *Rodolfo Luis Jimenez Anaya Rodolfo Luis Jimenez Anaya Rodolfo Luis Jimenez Anaya Rodolfo Luis Jimenez Anaya.* I take one more hit from the translucent red bottle and whisper, "Enough."

I shut my eyes until the world becomes a softer place, liquid and easy. "Anna is loyal," I slur. "Loyal." Maybe we're in a tough spot at the moment, but she loves me and I love her and neither of us are quitters. It's all good. Everything's all right. A-Okay. "We were made for one another."

Soon I'm floating like a sea otter, adrift with my hands on my belly, going up and over, up and over each gentle swell.

I wake with a sense of foreboding, willing my eyes to open. It's not a bear but a large man in a brown suit. He's striding across the lawn toward me. He's not smiling. Fear flashes through me as I fight through layers of clouds inside my head, trying to understand this new reality. I consider leaping to my feet and running away, but at the same moment, know that this isn't possible. My limbs weigh a thousand pounds.

I call out to him, "Wait!"

He stops, but just for a moment, and then he's coming at me again. I start to pull myself toward the bus stop, but he's here, standing over me with a quizzical, only slightly alarmed, look. I think of the big black bear I once passed on the Coastal Trail.

"Hold on," I say. My tongue is sluggish and dry. Where am I? The Hillside? "I am so sorry."

"Are you all right?"

The sky is gray, but a bright gray, a blinding gray. I blink against it as I look up at him. The man is about sixty, his face ruddy and pockmarked, silver hair sprouting from his nose. Okay, okay. He must be a husband. Even in this modern age, we rarely meet the husbands. "Oh, hello Mr., um?"

"Jim."

Jim? Which one is Jim? It was Anna's idea to never call clients by their first names, always their last preceded by Mr. or Ms. (pronounced mzzz, she insists, and never ever miss or missus).

"Mr. Calhoun, sir, I'm so sorry. I'm Henry, your housecleaner. I guess I fell asleep waiting for the bus."

He laughs and crouches by me. "What? You fell clear asleep? The grass is all wet. You must be working too hard, pal."

"Guess I missed my bus."

"Look, how about I run you home? I gotta hit the store anyway."

In the passenger seat of his brand-new fiery orange Toyota Tacoma, I do my best to talk about the Seahawks' last season. I don't give a shit about sports, but in the event of a husband ambush, it's my job to deal with him. Sports are always a safe bet. Anna takes charge of the wives, who are more difficult because they come with an agenda, showing us the streaks on a bureau mirror or a small rug we forgot to shake out. The strategy Anna uses on the wives is to knock them off course with a cascade of personal questions. Caught off-guard, I've seen her simply grab a photo off the mantel and say, "Now who is this cutie pie?" Anna is a true professional.

"Have time for a beer, Henry?"

We are on the highway, speeding toward town. The name *Rodolfo Luis Jimenez Anaya* shoots through my mind like an angry poem, and my stomach turns over. "Couldn't hurt, right?"

He chuckles and guns the engine. Of course, the last thing I want right now is to talk to a husband. A beer might help me out, though. Plus, there is the referral to think about. Anna says that if our clients are home, we should make ourselves into whatever it is they want: buddies, confessors, surrogate children. Most of the time I enjoy playing the role. I think, deep down, Anna does too.

Mr. Calhoun pulls into the packed parking lot of a sports bar. I ride past this place on my bike all the time, the faux log cabin exterior beneath a giant satellite dish. Although I hate all sports bars, along with the illiterate idiots who pack the places, it occurs to me that I might be hungry. All I had today was a bowl of mushy organic cereal from my morning house. Maybe a burger will take up some of the hollow space within me.

As I get out of the truck, I decide that I need a minute to collect myself, so I tell Mr. Calhoun to head in and hold my phone up as explanation.

Instead of making a call, though, I take out the vial of Valium and turn it over and over in my palm. No, I shouldn't. Anna's show starts in less than an hour, and she would kick my ass from here to Nome. Anna.

I don't believe in God, I mean please, but when I hear the religious nuts talking about proof of God, I can't help but think of Anna. When she smiles, her eyes effervesce. Enthusiasm fizzes from the very center of her pupils. Imagine black champagne. I stow the Valium in my pocket and then touch the warm bright metal of the truck.

Is she sleeping with him? Could she be? I clamp a hand over my heart. Is my life already ruined, but she just hasn't let me know it yet? I think of the old Westerns where the cowboy gets an arrow through his chest and topples right off his horse. Wouldn't that be better than this slow torture?

I can imagine her doing something crazy and then regretting it. She's always been impulsive.

I think of the time we were posting flyers for our cleaning service around town, me on my mountain bike and Anna holding my seat post trailing behind me on Rollerblades. As we dropped down the hill toward L Street, Anna kept yelling at me to pedal faster. She never wore a helmet. I ignored her and continued to ease on the brakes as a truck roared beside us. We were closing in on the intersection at the bottom of the hill.

"Come on, Henry! We can make the light!" she yelled.

I shook my head, clamping down harder on the brakes. Anna glided up a few inches, right next to me, and crouched like a speed skater. Next thing I knew, she was sailing down the hill alone. I wouldn't have been more shocked if she'd taken flight. My vision narrowed, became tunnel-like, as she shot into the busy intersection. She made it to the other side, car horns blaring, and raised her fist high into the air.

Impulsive. Maybe that's part of what draws me to her?

Inside the restaurant, we order some beers and then cheeseburgers and Cajun wings. The Cubs are playing on the monitors above our heads.

"So, where's your girl today, Henry?"

"A show. She's got an art opening tonight."

"That so? Art, huh, like who is it? Picasso?"

"Not exactly. She's a photographer."

"Oh, okay, pictures." He nods his head, inexplicably pleased with this news. "She has something else going on, picture-taking. I got a niece does that, weddings mostly. Makes out okay, believe it or not."

Anna would rather clean toilets than do wedding shoots, but I keep it to myself.

"So how about you, kiddo?"

"Um . . . ?"

The server sets our pints down, one after the other, tan froth running over her hand and spilling onto the table. Mr. Calhoun raises his glass to her and says, "Here's to you, gorgeous."

I suppose she is pretty, her bleach blonde hair up in a messy bun. She gives him a tight smile, and when she turns to me, I roll my eyes. I want her to understand that I am nothing like him, but I work for him so I can't let him know it. Is it just my imagination or does her smile widen just a bit?

Mr. Calhoun sighs, watching her walk away. "I think she's got the hots for you, kiddo. What I wouldn't do to be your age again. What are you, twenty-one? Twenty-two?"

"Twenty-four."

"Twenty-four years old." He whistles and shakes his head. "By that age, I had two kids and a wife. Not Melinda, I mean my first wife. God, what piece of work she was! I thought I was marrying a beautiful Swede, but she turned out to be a goddamn Viking." He shivers and downs half his pint.

I don't know how to respond. I'm not used to talking to the husbands. Thankfully, he turns to watch the Cubs take the field above my head. I tap my fingers on the vial in my jacket pocket. Just the touch of the warm plastic gives me a feeling like I can handle whatever shit comes my way. Or maybe whatever shit doesn't come my way? I think of the bumper sticker I saw earlier this summer on a VW campervan: WANT LESS, SUFFER LESS.

Mr. Calhoun probably thinks I'm a screwup—most of the husbands do—but man! I would never trade my life for his. Ex-wives and kids and mortgages and tuitions and layaways and 401Ks. As far as I can tell, my clients are all miserable. Maybe I am, too, but at least my misery doesn't cost so much. Or reproduce itself. I've met one of Mr. Calhoun's boys, who has all the personality of a microwave burrito. One day I was vacuuming the family room while the lump sat there swearing at his video game, and all I could think was, *His parents work their lives away for this little turd? Forget it!* I agree with the old hippies. Tune in, and drop out.

Anna does not like my philosophy. She's always on me to move up in the world. How ironic that stealing drugs was her idea, at least initially. We had been in business almost a year when she found out she had been rejected for a big local grant. She didn't seem upset when she read the email, but later that afternoon, cleaning a beautiful log home just off O'Malley Road, she plopped down on the couch and started in with *Judge Judy*. I was getting irritated doing all the work myself, but after a couple of hours she came into the master bath grinning and shaking a brown plastic vial at me.

By the next week, we were popping pills in every house. Codeine, Demerol, Stadol, Vicodin. It's amazing how overprescribed old rich people are. They never seem to finish the course of their drugs, and yet they never throw them out. I thought it strange that they kept the motherlode of pills in the kitchen rather than the bathroom, until Anna pointed out the labels: *Take with food.*

When the server returns with our plates, I give her an apologetic smile, hoping Mr. Calhoun keeps himself in check. He only has eyes for those buffalo wings, though. He tucks a napkin into his T-shirt and goes right at them, orange buffalo sauce all down his chin and hands, his lips shiny with the grease. He's not supposed to be eating or drinking like this—his wife told me about his ulcer.

I take a bite of my burger, but I suddenly lack the will to chew it. I should be hungry after cleaning all day on empty. I shift the doughy bun and charred meat from one side of my dry mouth to the other. What I need is a hit of the Valium in my pocket.

"So, Henry," Mr. Calhoun says, at last taking a break from his wing frenzy, "your girl has her picture business, you got anything going?"

I shrug. "I don't know. I guess I do art, too, or I used to anyway. In fact, that's how I met Anna. We were in the same program at school."

He sits back in his chair, a look of wonder on his face. "No shit?"

"Yep."

"You take pictures?"

"No, I do sculpture."

"Well, what do you know? Sculpture? Like statues and things?"

"I upcycle."

He takes a long swallow of beer and then waits for an explanation with a patient frown.

"It's like recycling but for a higher purpose. I find scrap metal and old batteries and junk parts and use it as my raw material."

"Hold on a minute, pal. Are we talking about garbage here?"

"Well, I wouldn't use the word *garbage*."

"Go figure. Now I've heard it all." A thought comes over him, and he chuckles. "Hey, I guess it's true what they say, one man's trash is another man's treasure?"

The wave of boredom that has been building within me now crashes. I am so filled with restlessness that I start counting my fries. This has been happening lately. It's like my soul is trapped in a cast, and there's no way out. I try to conjure my old self, the guy who would stay up all night drinking Red Bull in his dorm and working tin cans onto coat hangers as though the world depended on his art. Where did all that inspiration go?

"So," Mr. Calhoun says, mopping at his big ruddy face with a napkin. "Let me ask you, Henry. Do people buy these garbage statues?"

The one bite of burger sits like a rock in my stomach. "Well, not so much. It was never about the money, though."

He turns this over in his mind for a while with a somewhat pained expression on his face. Then he leans in and, in a cautious voice, says, "Pal?"

"Yeah?"

"*Everything* is about the money."

I glance at the TV screen. A player is sliding into second but gets tagged out.

"Don't you ever think about your future, Henry?"

"Not really."

He leans back in his chair, his lump of belly fat straining the buttons on his shirt. "But you went to college, right? Jeez. I just barely made it through high school, and look at me now."

I smile, reaching down to feel the pills in my pocket. "Yeah well, Anna and I graduated in '07. Right in time for the recession."

"Recession? Haven't you taken a look around? Up in Alaska we're going gangbusters, kid."

Anna says the same thing every time I point out how most of our friends back home are living with their parents. She thinks I'm not trying hard enough. As though cleaning all those big houses were easy.

The server comes over to clear our plates. She really is pretty. I throw a napkin over my nearly untouched burger and smile up at her as she balances the plate on her arm. She takes my glass, and her fingers touch mine for a moment.

"You all set here? Another amber?"

"No," I say, and no is what I'm thinking. No, no, no. I could never love her. She might as well be a mannequin. There is no sense of infinity in her flat blue eyes, no feeling stirring in me like a door opening onto a door opening onto a door. With Anna, there is always another door to open.

I rub my face, and then hold my hands there. What am I going to do? She doesn't love me anymore. I can't just sit here, waiting for the check to come, pretending my life isn't over. My heart starts thumping. It feels like a wild bird caught in my chest.

Mr. Calhoun clears his phlegm-filled throat. "Henry, I think I understand where you're coming from."

I peer through my fingers at him.

He leans back in his chair, not in any hurry to leave this place. "You're young. You make enough money for beer and movies, and you got a great girl. But you have to start thinking about tomorrow. Especially if you want to keep that girl." He snatches a napkin from the dispenser and blows his nose. "You know, here in Alaska they have their pick of us, kid. There's a saying that women here don't *break* up with you, they *trade* up on you."

She doesn't love me anymore. The thought mixes with the bile in my stomach. For months, she's been turning away from me, slowly, like a flower turns toward the brighter light. I'm worthless. I do nothing for her, have nothing to offer her. But then I think about last week when she came up behind me while I was making us lunch, and she lay her check on my shoulder and sighed. It was the good kind of sigh, like I'm starving and here you are making me a grilled cheese. A "what would I do without you?" sort of sigh. A "my hero" kind of deal. At least, I think it was.

I drop my hands to the table and say, "Anna's not like that."

"Listen, guy, they're *all* like that." He balls his napkin, then works an edge at the orange sauce encrusted in his fingernails. "I like you, Henry. You're a good kid, a nice kid. But you gotta wake up."

To the men's room, I think. My only hope. "Yessir. I think I see what you mean. Listen, I've got to take a leak. I'll be right back." I get up and then turn, forcing a smile. "And thank you so much for the burger and beer, Mr. Calhoun. And the ride, too. Really very cool of you. Super cool."

Super cool? I sound like an idiot. I'm glad Anna isn't here to witness it. She used to insist on over-the-top politeness, but then one day just scrapped it all, said she couldn't do it anymore. Now she talks like a Marxist.

In the stall, I open the bottle and shake out a couple of pills. They don't match, one is oblong and white, the other is round and red. A grab bag rather than straight up Valium, common but not always a good thing. There might be a bunch of antibiotics or over-the-counter buzzkills like Tylenol PM mixed in with the good stuff. I hold each pill close to read their tiny labels. My spirits lift, an OxyContin. I search through the rest of the pills, only a few of which are Valium. I dry swallow one and then wash my face in the sink.

Anna has changed. Up until last fall, when I was still doing my art, Anna used to hit the dumpsters with me. We would go on raids for my sculptures but also go by some restaurants and bakeries for their day-old food. She got freaked out one day waiting for the Fred Meyer bread dump when a whole family, little kids and all, lined up behind us. Later, on the bus to a cleaning job, she slumped against me, "Henry, did we just steal food from homeless people?"

"What? No! They had like a whole hefty bag for themselves." She didn't look convinced, so I added further consolation. "We're poor too."

"We're poor," she said, "but we're not *poor* poor."

"What's the difference? It's just free bread, Anna. They were throwing a ton of it away."

"Jesus, is this my life? Eating out of trash cans? Scrubbing toilets for a living?"

I felt a pressure building under my ribs. "Bathrooms are mine. You never get the grout clean."

She blinked her eyes at me, incredulous. "Do you understand where I'm coming from, Henry? My grandmother cleaned houses when she came to this country. And here I am in the same spot, serving rich fuckers."

"How can you say that, Anna? They're so good to us."

"They're the lords, and we're their servants!"

"We're small-business owners."

"No, Hen, we're maids."

When I didn't respond to this, she continued her tirade. "Is this how far I've gotten? Is this why I went to college?" And then she kicked our red bucket of cleaning supplies for emphasis.

It was as though she kicked me, too, right in my red heart. Bruised it with her Xtratufs, and this was months before Rodolfo Luis Jimenez Anaya came into our lives.

Back in the truck, Mr. Calhoun offers a sly smile. "How about we hit the Bush Company for one more round?"

"I should get to Anna's show, and I still have to go home to shower and stuff."

"Well, shit, Henry. I've never seen such a sorry case of P-whipped. Where am I taking you, then?"

I roll down the window a bit and feel fine as the air hits my face. *Rodolfo Luis Jimenez Anaya* trails through my mind, but I'm able to relax now and simply let the name keep on going right out the window. Hate, jealousy, fear—all going, going, gone.

"Well," Mr. Calhoun says, pulling up in front of our building. "It's past six. You're going to be late."

"Not by much."

He studies my face for a moment. "You okay, son?"

"Sure, I'm fine."

He doesn't look convinced. "Listen, I've got a few things to do, but I'd like to come by and see your girlfriend's pictures tonight, if you don't mind. Who knows? I might even buy one. Melinda goes in for all that art deco stuff."

"Sounds good, Mr. Calhoun. She would like that."

"Jim."

"Jim, then."

"You sure you're okay?"

"I'm great. Why?"

"I don't know. Your eyes look a little . . . well, hell, kid. You look like your poodle just croaked."

I take the Coastal Trail downtown, hoping the exercise will sober me up. I'm flying, pedaling hard, my eyes roving over the gray mudflats to the darker line of horizon. My head starts to ache, and soon a sinking, slippery feeling comes over me. Nothing in my life is solid. With each pedal rotation, a different thought churns through my brain. No health insurance. No savings. Student loans. Why is everything in Alaska so expensive? How can I be working so hard and still be sinking? Am I really any freer than Mr. Calhoun?

I seize the brakes. Breathing hard, I study the cracked gray flats that stretch out before me. I heard that years ago, a guy tried to take a walk out there. His feet got stuck, and the more he struggled, the deeper he sank. The tide comes in fast in Alaska, and even in the summer, the water is cold.

Rescue crews tied a rope to him and tried to haul him out, but the mud held like cement. There was nothing anyone could do but watch as the seawater rose over his head.

By the time I reach the warehouse, sweat is dripping from my underarms and I'm shivering. I stand outside the door for a while, combing my hands through my hair and wiping my face with the front of my T-shirt.

A bearded man in a battered Carhartt jacket walks past and then holds the door open. "You coming?"

Inside, I am struck by the bright white partitions on wheels arranged all across the room. The noise of a hundred conversations ricochets around the cavernous warehouse, and I fight the urge to run back outside. I scan the crowd, looking for him. Rodolfo Luis Jimenez Anaya. People swarm about the warehouse laughing, sipping wine, in constant motion. They all seem so carefree. A short woman carrying an oversized Nalgene bottle and a small camera is taking pictures of the crowd. I wonder who all of these people are? What do they do for a living? Do they have 401Ks? All I want is to get on my bike and pedal up into the mountains.

Anna appears. It's as though she has dropped down from the ceiling, mobbing me with her arms, alternately hugging and violently shaking me. She has such strong arms for a girl.

"Ow."

"You're so late, Henry. I can't believe this. I mean, it's my opening."

"Sorry, I got a flat."

Her fingers dig into my arm. "Nobody was here! The place was empty for so long!"

"There are tons of people here."

"Well, they all came in the last fifteen minutes. I've been freaking out!" She presses close against me and I catch the lovely scent of her hair—sharp as lemon rinds—and study her face, a beautiful rose spreading from each of her cheeks. But the look in her eye is broken. No fizz of champagne. "It's like you don't care about anything anymore. Not even me."

"That's totally not true."

"And you look like shit. Are you on something?"

"No!" I look away, combing down my hair with my fingers. "I've been working all day, and then I rode here. Sorry if I don't exactly fit in with the gentry."

"Gentry?" She stands back on a heel, scrutinizing me, and then throws up her hands. "Okay, you're here."

"Yes, I am. So how about showing me your pictures?"

She points from one wall to the other as though directing me to the bathroom. "There's no particular order to the show. You can start anywhere."

"Aren't you going to stay with me?"

"Hen, I have exactly half an hour left to try to sell this work and actually make some money. So, no. You're a big boy. You'll manage."

I watch her walk away, her tight beige skirt hugging her hips and ass. Where did that outfit come from? I've never seen her wear it before. The fact that it looks so good on her only pisses me off more.

I take another slow glance around the room, but nobody fits my image of Rodolfo Luis Jimenez Anaya, so I step up to the closest photograph. It's a black-and-white shot of someone's leg, a woman's. Her thigh is all covered in mud, you can just make out the triangle of dark hair, half out of the frame. An eerie feeling spreads from my stomach. The next shot shows a small clean hand clasped in between two mud-crusted breasts, and I stand back to take in the whole line of photographs, "What the hell?"

It's her. Anna. Every single picture.

"Powerful, yes?" A big guy in a black suit smiles down at me. He has a crooked nose, heavy eyebrows, and the chest-forward stance of a boxer. Rodolfo Luis Jimenez Anaya. My breath catches in my throat, and my heart jackhammers. This is it. Right now.

"Incredible what she does with tone. Rodolfo, by the way, and you are Henry? Pleased to meet you at long last."

I blink. I've never been in a real fight before. As a kid, I was beaten up somewhat regularly, but this situation feels very different. The room, unlike the schoolyard, lacks a sense of violence. It's too civilized here. Already the anger is draining from me, threatening to turn to tears. Maybe if we were out on the street?

But then Anna is there between us. "So, what do you think?"

"What do I think?"

"Yes, Henry, about my exhibit? You know, the one Rodolfo and I have been working on like crazy for months and months?"

It all comes back to me then, a tsunami of pure hatred. "Rodolfo Luis Jimenez Anaya," I say, "let's go. Outside."

"Outside?" He turns from me to Anna for confirmation.

"Outside!"

I glare at him, hot tears of anger stinging my eyes.

"Maybe I should get him a glass of water?" Rodolfo suggests to Anna.

"Come on!" I yell, and in two strides I am at the door, holding it open for him.

But it isn't Rodolfo Luis Jimenez Anaya who passes me. It's Anna. As she does, she takes hold of my wrist and pulls me behind her.

"He was there with you, wasn't he?" I yell as the door begins to swing shut. I kick it, directing all my hatred through my foot to the point of contact on the door. It's an industrial push-bar steel door, much heavier than I anticipated. Pain shoots up my leg despite the cough syrup and Valium, and now I'm limping, doing my best to keep up with her furious pace.

When we hit the walkway, she turns to face me. "What the hell are you talking about?"

"You know exactly what I'm talking about. Him."

"Him, who? And goddamn it, Henry, you are high! You're high as a kite!"

"Just tell me the truth about him?"

She shook her head as though to clear it. "About Rodolfo? What?"

"Was he there with you when you created that—that pornography?"

The word hangs in the air, and her eyes go wide. All life on planet Earth stills.

"Okay, Henry," she says from across a thousand-foot chasm, "I'm going back in to my life now. Good-bye."

I run my hands down my jacket and pull on the busted zipper. Words that should come, don't. I can only watch as, frame-by-frame, she salutes, spins on a high heel, and starts walking away from me.

When she is nearly through the door, I rouse as though from a nightmare. "I love you!"

She pauses, holding two beautiful fingers to her forehead. She is framed by the gallery door and, beyond it, the jagged tips of the Chugach peaking above their misty cover. I think, *This is a moment I will remember all my life. The story we'll tell our grandchildren.*

But then she is gone.

The street is silent by the railroad, and the only sound is my ragged breathing. I bury my face in my hands. After some time, I look back to the gallery, hoping to see Anna coming back out to me, calling, *I love you too, Hen!*

What I see instead is the cut chain underneath the street sign where I locked my bike.

Sinking to the curb, I lay my head on my knees and weep. I cry and cry, blubbering until my throat aches.

Somebody gently touches the back of my neck, and I lift my head. "Anna?"

But no. Mr. Calhoun's fleshy red face is drawn with concern. "Hey pal," he says, taking a labored seat next to me on the curb. "You don't even have to say it. I know. I know. Your girl left you, huh?"

I nod, smearing tears and snot along my face with my sleeve.

He picks up the chain at my feet. "And what the hell is this? Your bike got stolen too?"

Sniffing, I take the chain from him and run my fingers over the sharp metal of the break.

"Well, isn't that a shit show for you? Just how much do they expect a man to take in one night?"

More tears well in my eyes.

"Ah, hell, kid. I am sorry." We sit in silence for some time, and then he takes a deep breath and clasps me on the back. "Well, I'll tell you what. I am taking your sorry ass directly to the closest titty bar and getting you drunk to the tops of your eyeballs and then some."

This is the last place I want to go right now, but his hand feels reassuring on my back. I'm glad he's here with me. "Mr. Calhoun?"

"Jim."

"Jim, would you stay here with me for a while?"

Just then, on the far side of the building, a moose steps out from the shadows. His antlers flare with just three points a side, a young bull.

"How about that?" Mr. Calhoun says.

Closer and closer the bull approaches, a huge, shaggy, gangly thing, until he is right before us, his breath just visible in the wet chilly air. I'm too shocked to be afraid. He knocks his antlers against the street sign, leaving a strip of velvet, and moves along the sidewalk, giving several shakes of his head as though he's in pain.

Mr. Calhoun looks through the scope of an imaginary rifle. "Kapow! One for the stew pot."

I continue to watch the animal. He looks so out of place here, like some mythical beast from an ancient time, a unicorn or Pegasus. I wonder where he's going? Does he have any idea himself? The young bull shakes his head once more, takes a few disjointed steps off the curb, and begins to make his graceless way down the middle of the street.

"Well, kid," Mr. Calhoun says. "What's next?"

WEATHERED IN

BREAKUP

I wanted to have the flu. All of the clues told me otherwise, but I believed what I needed to believe. If I had the flu, I would soon be done with it and be able to join Karl and the rest of our group on the Denali climb. We'd been in Talkeetna for the better part of a week, sleeping in the back of our aging red Toyota named Yo, because most of the letters on the tailgate had weathered away leaving only these two letters between the brake lights. Yo was already an old lady when we bought her in Bozeman, but we managed to keep her running through all the years and mountain states by treating her like our beloved, though quirky, grandmother. Every time we had to get her up to speed or altitude, Karl would open her hood and talk gently right into her engine. I loved listening to him cajole the old truck into good behavior. "You've been with Rachel and me a long time, baby," he would say. "Through thick and thin, ice and rain, and I don't care about the big number on the odometer, you can still turn headlights."

My father worried about our lifestyle, of course. We had just wrapped up two years in various towns in Colorado, couch surfing or living in our truck while Karl earned a graduate degree in engineering. I supported us on my meager coffee shop wages and a side business of combing thrift stores for good quality gear and clothing, then reselling. Now we were in our tumbleweed phase, which was really not so different from our grad school phase. Karl charmed and begged his way through the program, and we spent more time on the road and in the mountains than in the classroom. I had a small inheritance from my mother who had died two years before, but we barely touched the money because we knew how to live cheaply: oatmeal for breakfast, peanut butter for lunch, rice and beans for dinner. Our biggest expense was coffee, beer, and weed because we only bought the highest quality of each.

My dad thought I should be building a career of my own. He struggled with getting me into college, and he simply couldn't fathom why I wasn't using my degree. "Rachel," he was always saying, "climbing is a leisure time activity. A hobby. You can't center your whole life around it."

That, however, was exactly what Karl and I were doing. We lived simply and in the moment, and though my dad couldn't accept this, I thought my mother would have been happy for me. "Live your entire life while you're young," she used to say.

We drove to Alaska in April, taking our time to do some climbs in Oregon and Washington. I wasn't prepared for spring in the Far North. There was still snow on the ground at sea level. Lots of it. Every morning when we hiked to the café in Talkeetna, the snow crust held our weight, but by the time we turned back our feet postholed through the snow, wetting our pants up past our knees.

"We don't call it spring," said Sara, the barista. "Alaska doesn't really get spring, not like you do Outside. We call it breakup."

"Breakup?" I asked.

"Yeah, when the ice on the rivers and lakes breaks up."

"And that happens in April?"

"Or May. Depends on what part of the state you're in, really. And what the weather feels like doing," she laughed. "Like this year, we've had more snow than ever! Alaska does what it wants, and we just have to deal with it."

I liked Sara. She was my age and had a college degree but served coffee for a living. She wasn't a climber, which surprised me because Talkeetna was a small town with a big climbing reputation. It's the jumping-off point for

Denali and other peaks in the Alaska Range. When I commented on this, she shook her head and said she'd been there long enough to get scared.

"Denali's not a hard climb," she said. "On a nice day, the final push is just a hike up to the summit. Problem is, there's not too many nice days." She poured herself a cup of coffee and set it on the counter next to my chamomile tea. "I've seen lots of bad trouble."

"Like what?"

"Climbers who, you know, they're still up there." She took a drink of her coffee, then laid her hand on mine. "I guess the number one lesson Alaska taught this cheechako is to be careful."

"Cheechako?"

"That's what Alaskans call newcomers. But why am I going on about this? You're experienced. You know what you're in for."

I nodded and glanced back to Karl sitting at our table. "Seems to me the problem with Denali is that it's a tourist destination. Lots of people going up just to say they did it, and they don't know much at all about mountaineering. We usually stay away from those sorts of climbs."

"What made you decide to do it?"

"There's something special about Denali. It calls to me, and I don't really know why. I've wanted to climb it since I first started mountaineering."

"The High One," Sara said in a mocking tone. She took another sip of her coffee. "But I know what you're talking about. I live here at the foot of it, and I feel its presence every day. There is something . . . God-like about it."

"But you don't want to climb it?"

"You know, when I first got here an old-timer told me that the only reason he would climb Denali is if he left something up there and had to go back and get it."

"But how would he leave something up there if he never went up in the first place?"

Sara grinned at me.

"Okay, I get it." I drew my hand along the counter. "But seriously, you have no desire to climb it? None at all?"

"I guess I'm more inclined to drop to my knees before it."

"Quaking?"

"Yes, ma'am! Alaska has turned me into a god-fearing woman."

I woke up early with my stomach heaving the day before we were to fly to base camp. The roof of the truck's cap was dripping condensation onto our sleeping bags, and the windows were fogged over. I fumbled out of the pickup and got sick on the ice-glazed snowbank lining the camp.

I woke Karl, who dropped open the tailgate and blinked himself awake. "Still sick, huh?"

"I'll be okay," I said. He handed me a water bottle and I rinsed my mouth. "I'm actually feeling much better now."

"You don't look so good."

"Thanks."

"No, I mean you look really pale. Come on back to bed."

I shivered in the cold morning air, my breath a streaming cloud. Karl held open our joined sleeping bags, and the warmth of his bare chest and arms released the deep exhaustion in me. I lay against him and shut my eyes.

"I'm worried," he said.

"I'll be fine."

He was quiet for a while, but I knew he was studying me.

"I'm the group leader. And you know that means making lots of hard decisions," he said.

"What are you talking about?"

"Not going on the climb. Skipping this one."

"No way." I rose on an elbow. "We drove all the fucking way from Colorado. If we don't go tomorrow, we'll lose our window."

"I meant that you're not going."

"Because I puked a few times? I'm getting better!" I was glad I hadn't told him I might be pregnant. "Are you serious?"

"Look, Rachel," he said, pulling me against his warm chest. "It kills me to say this. But I just can't allow it. As the group leader, I can't bring a sick person up the mountain. End of story."

I pulled away from him. "This is bullshit!" The beat of anger made its way from my sour stomach up my neck to my head, where it throbbed. My hands clenched into tight fists and I fought the impulse to punch him. He wouldn't even look at me, the coward. "Who made you the leader anyway?"

"I don't know. It was my idea, my trip from the start. I got the boys together."

"The boys!" I yanked the zipper open. "You can't just make a decision like this without talking to Dave and everybody."

"I already did."

I turned away from him, furious that he would go behind my back like that. Anger was no longer the right word. What I felt was betrayal. I studied the drops of condensation racing down the pane. "What if it was you?" I asked. "What if you were a little under the weather, and I was barring you from the climb?"

"But I never get sick."

He was right. He never did, whereas every winter I came down with several colds and sometimes the flu. When we traveled overseas, I was always the one who became ill with what we called "mystery maladies." His body was better able to endure extreme cold, as well. Last year weathered in at high altitude, the tips of three of my fingers went black with frostbite, and though our exposure, caloric intake, and quality of gear were the same, he came off the mountain in fine shape.

"I'm going on the climb," I told him.

"You're not just a little under the weather, Rachel. You've barely eaten a thing since we got here." He ran his hands through his shaggy hair. "I'm almost thinking I should bow out too. But I'm the group leader, and I don't want to ruin it for everybody. Plus, Sara said she'd watch out for you."

"You talked to Sara already? Before saying any of this to me?"

"I know we just met her and all, but she's super nice. Maybe you can even stay at her place?"

I refused to respond. My anger took a sharp turn inward.

That night the guys partied it up at camp. They knew enough to leave me alone. Even Sara, after handing me a hot mug of tea, retreated after sensing my mood. I liked her, but I didn't know her that well. I didn't want to stay with her for a whole month with nothing to do. I considered simply leaving, doing solo hikes and climbs. I even thought about taking off for good.

I pulled on my high rubber boots and walked down to the river with my toothbrush. I had to admit we found a nice camp spot right near the bank. After brushing my teeth, I began to retrace my boot prints back to camp, and I came across a huge brown bear track in the snow. For some reason just one was discernible, but it was perfect, the colder night preserving it with a hard rime. I was going to call out so Karl could see it, but then I thought, *Screw him!*

Back in the truck, I was glad for the river because the revelers were still cracking beers around the fire, and the current drowned out their voices. Like staring into flames, listening to a river is hypnotizing. Rhythmic spaces separated the riffles of sound and in those spaces, thoughts came to me, fleeting and sharp. There was an image of a bundle wrapped in a bright blue tarp, strapped with bungee cords. A raven was perched on top, bending a quizzical eye to the bundle and giving an occasional sharp peck at a flap of the tarp. Even in my dream, I knew what lay within. I'd seen it. On our last trip to China. Under the tarp was the body of a frozen climber.

When I awoke, my face was wet with tears. I was startled to find Karl next to me. He put his arms around me. "You know I'm agonizing about this," he whispered. "Will you ever forgive me?"

I was shivering in my sleeping bag, the dream still with me. "It's not just that I want to go. I have a bad feeling about us splitting up like this. About you going up alone."

He began to kiss my hair and face. "I won't be alone."

"I mean without me."

"Why?"

"I don't know. Just a feeling, I guess. We should stick together."

"You don't trust my judgment?"

I looked away.

"Okay," he said, "you might be more conservative than I am, but I'm not stupid. Don't I always end up agreeing with you in the end?"

"But if I'm not there, that's what worries me."

He hugged me close. "I'll be back down in no time. You'll see."

We were quiet for a while, and I felt his body relax against mine.

"Karl?"

"Hmmm?"

"All of our friends have dogs. Why did we never get one?"

He turned and looked at me. "Are you kidding? A *dog*? *Us*?"

"Yeah. Why?"

"Um—because we suck . . ." Karl yawned and pulled the cap lower on his forehead.

"Last year we killed a cactus. Remember?"

I nodded. It was after a trip to Peru. We came home to find our flowering green plant a desiccated brown, the petals reduced to chaff, only the translucent needles still looked healthy. At the time we found it funny, cacti generally not needing much care. But now I wasn't so sure.

In the morning, I clambered out of the truck and didn't even make it to the snowbank, hurling beside the rear wheel.

"And good morning to you!" Karl's just-awake voice was more buoyant than usual, and then I remembered why. Soon he would fly out.

I ignored him and sucked in long draughts of cold air. It made me feel better. My sense of smell, I noticed, was more powerful than before, and I could differentiate the clean scent of snow from the woody birches or the almost metallic river water from the moldy scent of last fall's mashed leaves. Breathing it all in ushered forth an odd sense of health and well-being. I'd forgotten what that felt like, and I was almost dizzy from the surge.

This was not the flu. A raven hopped down from a low pine branch, waddled closer to me, cocked his head in question, took a few more steps, then cocked his head again. I looked right into his black eyes. They had no pupils and were covered by a filmy blue sheen, each of which mirrored my reflection. In China I really had seen the tarp-covered corpse, but there hadn't been a bird. The group of climbers was lowering the body down a steep ascent, too high even for a raven.

The same eerie feeling I experienced then came back to me now.

I drove Karl to the airstrip, pulled him close, and kissed him good-bye. I wanted to say something to him, to tell him that he wasn't safe without me. But I stayed quiet until he was climbing in the plane, a de Havilland Beaver, and then I yelled, "I love you!"

"I love *you*," he called back.

Driving away, it occurred to me that we were no longer kids. Both of us would be thirty in a few years. Was it strange we never discussed marriage? We sometimes talked about the faraway future, taking it for granted that we would be together, but never marriage and definitely not children.

I drove to the café, and Sara waved me to the front of the line. A bearded and bespectacled guy in a flannel shirt started to complain, but Sara snapped at him, "She just got cut out of her trip up the mountain, so cram it!"

He looked at me and nodded in empathy.

"What'll it be?" Sara asked. "Peppermint or chamomile?"

"I miss caffeine," I said. "But I know I won't be able to stomach it."

"Poor you. No caffeine, no alcohol. It's like you're preggers."

I felt the heat rise up my neck to my cheeks.

"Oh my God," she cried. She threw her dish towel onto the counter and came around to give me a hug. "Have you peed on a stick? Been to the clinic? Do you know for sure?"

I shook my head as tears ran down my cheeks.

"Karl doesn't know?"

"No."

She dragged me to sit at a table. The three men waiting in line for coffee made their way out the door. "I get off at two. I'll go with you to find out for sure." She hesitated, then drew a finger up my arm. "But if you are, is it a good thing or a bad thing?"

"I don't know." I grew calm, feeling like I was talking about somebody else.

The clinic in Talkeetna was empty. Soon it would be busy with victims of frostbite, edema, and other assorted climber problems. The nurse who took my blood was my age and a friend of Sara's.

"Joan will take good care of you," Sara said. She led me down the hall, smiling back at me with concern.

I thought I would have to wait a day or two for the results, but when Joan came back into the room, her beautiful round face softened once again into a concerned smile. "You are pregnant," she said. "And I am here to help you in any way I can. Questions, discussions, you name it."

I studied the Band-Aid on my arm, the dot of deep red blood in the very center. I couldn't think of anything to say.

"I'm understanding this wasn't planned," she said, taking a seat on the stool next to the examining table. "Is that right?"

I flexed my arm, the Band-Aid stretching my skin, and nodded. I needed to get outside.

"Do you want to take some time with this?"

"I think so," I said, standing up.

"Okay, just know that I'm here if you have any questions or want to discuss options."

I thanked her and hurried to collect my things. In the lobby, Sara took one look at me and then turned to Joan, taking several pamphlets from her. Outside, we argued about who would drive the few miles back to town, and she only backed down after I climbed into the driver's seat and strapped my belt across my chest. But I didn't start the engine. We just sat in the truck, and then I laid my arms and head on the steering wheel. "Karl and I couldn't even raise a cactus."

She put a hand to my back.

"We got a cactus for Christmas, went on a climb, and when we got back," I shrugged.

"But would you leave a baby and go off for weeks."

"We couldn't. I think that's my point," I said. I wished my mother was still alive. She loved babies and was the type you couldn't have a conversation with in a restaurant or plane if there was an infant nearby. I had the sense, though, that right now she would have offered me no direction at all but would've simply let me talk. It occurred to me that this was exactly what Sara was doing.

"Thanks," I said.

"No worries."

I leaned back and turned the ignition. "It's not exactly the end of the world, right?"

"Right," she said.

"There could be worse things."

"True."

I dropped the truck into gear and stepped on the gas. When we got to her cabin, though, I didn't want to go in. I explained that I needed to be alone for a while.

"Okay, but you're coming back for dinner," she said. "And you're staying here with me until the guys come back."

"Yes, ma'am!" I saluted her and then gave her a hug. "Thank you," I said, the words coming out too quickly.

"You'd do the same for me."

I hoped I would have, but I wasn't so sure. Karl and I had never led a settled life, the kind most people have with neighbors and friends. We would hit a new town and head for the mountains. It was nothing for us to quit our jobs, pull up stakes, say our good-byes. There was a set of people who came in and out of our lives, all mountaineers, but friendship only occurred in the context of a climb. The only constants I had in my life were Karl and the mountains. Now I thought about what I would have done if Sara was pregnant and had been cut out of the climb. I hated to admit this, but I most likely would have asked about taking her place on the team.

I pulled over and laid my head on the wheel once again. When I looked out the window, a thin church spire split the blue sky. Talkeetna was a drinking town full of bars, and I hadn't, up to this point, noticed any churches. I opened the truck door and stepped out for a breath of air.

I found myself walking up the few stairs to the heavy wooden doors. Once inside the chapel, I stood to one side, afraid to go any farther. The church smelled musty, like incense and old lumber. I wasn't raised in any church, but I'd been in quite a few. I liked to visit them in our travels—churches, mosques, shrines. I never felt comfortable in any of them, but I was often drawn in.

On a Tuesday, I was surprised to see I wasn't alone. An elderly woman and a child were there in the back of the church with me. They looked to be Native, the woman in a shawl and large round eyeglasses and the little girl with great big cheeks and a shy smile.

I stood for a moment feeling like a tourist and then turned to leave. But the little girl was eyeing me. She kept smiling and then dipped her head. What did she want? Next she moved her hand slyly from chest to shoulder to shoulder. She repeated, dipping her forehead for a touch of her fingers, then proceeding in the sign of the cross. Her grandmother, oblivious to me, was doing the same, but facing a large picture on the wall of Jesus surrounded by weeping women, a station of the cross.

The little girl giggled, pressing herself into her grandmother's shawl, but continued making the sign of the cross, her hand motions even more pronounced. I smiled back and crossed myself, but she frowned and shook her head. She raised her eyebrows to the picture on the wall.

I turned to the weeping women and repeated the cross more slowly; forehead, heart, shoulder to shoulder. I glanced back at the girl, and she beamed with such pride that I struggled to keep a solemn face. She thought she taught me something.

When I reached Sara's cabin, I found her out on the porch, playing the fiddle. I had to walk around a large puddle covering her entire front yard. The air was chilly, and Sara played a fiddle with fingerless gloves. Her breath rose in clouds above her head, as if the notes were taking flight.

Her eyes were shut, but when she finished the tune, she smiled at me and packed her instrument away. Sara had long, springy curls that seemed an extension of her soul. They bounced around her face.

She took my hand in both of hers, and I considered that under different circumstances, it would have taken us months to establish this sort of intimacy. But I was grateful. I couldn't imagine what I would be going through right then without her.

Sara's cabin was twelve feet by twenty-four, with a partial loft just big enough for her bed and dresser. She didn't own it but was renting from an ex-boyfriend. She pushed a steaming bowl of potato soup into my hands and indicated that I take a seat on the lumpy futon couch.

"Do you think it's a girl or a boy?" Sara asked.

"Look, I haven't really decided yet."

"Well, I hope it's a girl."

"I mean I haven't decided what I'm going to do."

"Oh, I'm sorry," she said. She put her bowl on the plywood coffee table and turned to face me, waiting.

"What?"

"It's just that I got the sense this afternoon that you did decide."

"Well, you were wrong," I looked away, sorry for the tone in my voice. The far wall was hung with climbing gear, looped bright blue and yellow nylon ropes, two harnesses, and an ice axe. On the other side of the door was Sara's kitchen. A double Coleman stove sat on a plywood countertop with a large red cooler underneath. I turned to look out the back window and saw the crisp half-moon cut into the outhouse door.

"How could I have a baby?"

"Why not?"

"No running water. That's one reason."

"You have running water. You run down to the river and get it."

I shook my head, but I was smiling. The rich earthy smell of the soup took hold of my senses as I stirred the spoon through thick broth. My appetite had come back in a new way, and I savored the warm, rooty potato flavor and spicy black pepper, but it was the salt that made me shut my eyes. Like a drug, the salt.

"Reason two," I said. "I live in a truck."

"Yes, you do. But you do it by choice. You and Karl live in that truck because you want to, and you know it."

She was right, of course. But it seemed worse that we chose to live this way. Like there was something wrong with us, something spoiled or stunted. I thought of the young woman I met in Tanzania who laughed at me for climbing up a mountain. *If I were an American*, she said, sucking in her breath and smiling, *I'd sit all day long drinking tea in the lobby of the finest hotel in Dar es Salaam. Why make work for yourself?* Like my father, she asked the sort of questions that I couldn't answer without sounding trite and flippant. But the only reason I could supply was that I lived how I did because I felt like it.

"Reason three," I said.

Sara waited, putting down her empty bowl. "Well?"

"I don't know. I haven't even told Karl. I don't know how he'll react."

"Maybe you should figure out what you feel, first."

I put my bowl down next to hers, feeling hot in the small cabin. "I need to get outside for a while."

We walked down the quiet evening streets of Talkeetna, where there were more dogs milling about than people. The sun was bright on my face, the evening sky clear. Denali rose in the distance, sharp-edged, covered in brilliant white and shadowed snow. I pictured Karl up there, setting up at base camp, sorting gear, or starting dinner. What was I going to do with myself in Talkeetna for three weeks? And when he returned, what then?

I noticed that sometimes Denali loomed large, even at this distance. Tonight though, the mountain appeared in perfect miniature. I stopped and held my hands around the image. The mountain fit easily between my palms.

"You worried about him up there?" Sara asked.

"No." I dropped my hands, releasing the mountain. "I'm worried about me being down here."

"I have an idea," Sara said, clutching my arm. "Let's go to the river."

We postholed our way to a bend where the bank spread wide and flat, and was littered with exposed driftwood. Whole trees had been weathered the color of rawhide with limbs stretching skyward from the snow.

"God's sculptures!" Sara spread her hand slowly in front of herself.

"Tree cemetery," I said, though I had to admit they were beautiful. I took a seat on one. The sun was hot on my face and my chapped lips burned. Maybe it was the reflection off the snow, or perhaps just the contrast in temperature that made the sun feel so warm.

The river was broken up, but there were still massive chunks of ice flowing in it, bobbing and turning with a feminine grace that belied how deadly they could be.

"In Cordova," Sara said, "I was kayaking by the Miles Glacier when it calved."

"Calved?"

"A big chunk of glacier split off and crashed into the water. Massive waves hit me."

"What did you do?"

"Paddled and prayed. And swore a goodly amount," she laughed. "The thing to do is to take the waves head on and ride them out. In the end, that's what saved me."

We grew quiet on the thick trunk of white driftwood. I learned the proper way to respond to a calving glacier. I wished real life came with this sort of instruction.

"I'm getting burned," I said.

"Me, too. But I like it after that long, dark winter. In fact," Sara said, "I'm thinking of moving somewhere warm. Mexico, maybe. Or Morocco."

"Really?"

"Are you surprised?"

"But I thought you were here for good." I felt the sting of betrayal, though we had only just met. I hurried to say more. "I just mean you seem to love it here, the cold and everything. I thought you were here for good. Like, an Alaskan."

She shrugged. "I've been here two winters now. They say if you last three, you stay."

"And?"

"And I don't know if I want to do that, to become Alaskan. I don't really want to become anything."

We laughed, but I knew what she meant. "Me, neither." I watched as a truck-sized floe of ice appeared for just a moment and then sunk below the current. "I can't imagine being a mother. Just one day and bang, there it is for the rest of my life. My whole entire life."

We sat together for some time just listening to the ice crack its way downriver. Tears stung like acid on my sunburned skin.

Sara turned to me, then quickly stood up. "I have an idea."

I regarded her, rubbing my fleece-covered wrist across my face. Fleece doesn't absorb tears. "What?"

"Time for a bath," she said.

"In the river? Are you crazy?"

"Nope. We're going to luxuriate in the snow."

"A snow bath?"

"I call it the White Powder Wash. It's rejuvenating. Energizing." She tore off her jacket, waved it around her head, then threw it on a driftwood log. "One day every salon in the world will offer it."

I laughed and joined her, peeling off layers of Gore Tex and fleece. We arranged our clothes on the eroded pegs of our driftwood tree. The air was chilly, but the evening sun burned warm on my skin.

"Are you ready for your spa treatment?"

"I suppose it's too late to back out?"

"Come on," she screamed, doing a belly flop. I followed suit, sinking into the grainy, wet snow. The granules were thick and icy, like sandpaper, and so cold my breath caught in my lungs.

"This is cruddy snow!" I struggled to stand. "Hardly powder."

"You want the powder treatment, see me in March."

Just like a jump into glacier-fed water, my body refused to adjust—the constricted blood vessels searing with pain, my heart pumping, and lungs collapsing. When I could handle no more, not one fraction of a second, Sara leapt up and pulled on her boots. I rubbed my body with a polypro T-shirt, which served to wipe away the snow but failed to dry me. I pulled my clothes over my wet skin, jumping up and down to get warm.

"Feel it yet?" Sara asked.

A flash of warmth and well-being ensued, and I hugged my arms around myself. I stood with closed eyes, my face angled to the sun. When I opened them, there was Denali, a forbidden kingdom floating above the distant clouds. It was suddenly hard for me to imagine Karl up there. Like a god, I thought. And I was down on the riverbed, a mere mortal.

MIDNIGHT SUN

I woke in the gray summer night, afraid. I heard it again, like distant thunder. Bolting upright in my sleeping bag, I soon understood that I was not in a tent on a mountain but in our truck. We were camping out at Eklutna Lake on our slow journey south. But my heart continued to race from the sound of the avalanche high up in the Chugach Mountains.

I looked down at Karl. He was awake too, smiling up at me from under the black skullcap he often wore to bed, but he looked rough. The weather at Denali's summit had slowed their ascent, and though they eventually made it to the top, their team took a beating. Karl's lips and chin were raw and blistered, and he'd lost weight. His bloodshot eyes looked huge in his thin face.

"Avalanches sound good when you're not in their path, huh?" he said.

I nodded, fear still squeezing my insides. Another one hit, closer this time, cracking lower down the mountain. Karl rubbed my back. He knew I was afraid, not exactly of avalanches, but more of being swept away by one in my sleep. He thought this was irrational, that being asleep would be a better way to go.

"Crazy that it's not dark yet," he said.

I checked my watch. "Yeah, it's almost eleven."

I'd been putting off telling Karl about the pregnancy. I didn't know why.

I was going to have it, so I wasn't worried about him pressuring me. He was the type who got excited about new ventures and projects, and unlike me, he loved surprises. But every time I started to tell him, I just couldn't. Maybe because the baby wasn't real to me until he knew.

"I'm thinking we mess around in the Chugach for a couple of weeks, then head to British Columbia and find some good technical climbs." Karl yawned as another avalanche slowly cracked the night, and I wondered if it was just my imagination or if I could actually make out the sound of individual trees being split in the forest on the lower mountain. "What do you think?" he said. "I know you're itching to get out now that you're over the flu."

"Karl, it wasn't the flu." I saw in the late light of the midnight sun how quickly his eyes shifted to me. He made no other movement, but his expression set with a particular intensity that I'd seen several times at altitude when unforeseen problems arise. I knew this to be his look of fear, his only concession to it.

"Okay, and can you tell me what's going on?" The words drawled slowly, his voice carefully pitched in curiosity rather than dread.

Another slide thundered from up high, and we listened to it cascade down into the forest. I was overcome by the sound of alders snapping like bones. "I'm pregnant."

"Oh, shit!" He sat up. "Jesus! I thought you were dying of something, cancer or some shit. You look so freaked out!" He laughed, pulled me close, his hands wrapping around my biceps. "A baby? Really?"

I nodded, bracing myself against his enthusiasm.

"This is a good thing!" He laughed again, crushing me against his stomach. "God, why were you so sneaky? How could you not tell me right away?"

I struggled to free myself. "I'm not sure we should be so happy about this."

"What are you talking about?"

"Karl, we live in a truck. Neither of us has a job. We killed a cactus last year."

"Well," he said, taking off his hat and scratching his head. "We'll just have to remember to water the kid!"

"And we don't know anything about babies. Not the first thing."

"How hard could it be? People have them all the time. We'll buy a manual or whatever." He leaned to unlatch the tailgate, then kicked it open. "Let's have a beer!"

I blinked at him in disbelief.

"Oh, that's right. I'll have to drink yours!"

When he crawled back into the truck, a water bottle for me, a warm, foaming bottle of Alaskan Amber for him, I said, "I'm serious, Karl. I'm not sure we're ready for this."

"You know, I was thinking just now. I like it up here. I like Alaska. Do you?"

"Yeah," I said. And I realized that I was telling the truth. Wherever you were in Alaska, even in the middle of a big city like Anchorage, you were surrounded by wilderness. I liked the feeling, how the wild mountains pressed in on you. "I guess I do."

He smiled and held my hand in his. "Then why don't we stay? We can find a place and jobs and all of that. We can even get married, if you want. And we'll raise the kid here."

I took a drink from the water bottle. "Stay here?"

"And the state even pays people to live here. It's like a thousand bucks for every man, woman, and child. Oil money, but what the hell. The little dude can pay for his own diapers!"

I lay down next to him and said nothing.

"What's going on with you?" he said after a while. "Aren't you even a little happy about this?"

An image filled my mind: hundreds of waxwings in a flock so dense they blocked out the sun. I saw them in Talkeetna soon after we arrived in April. They moved less like a flock of birds than a swarm of bees. Taking wing from several birch trees, a tight mass of fluttering confusion, they zoomed this way and that, settling back to perch for mere seconds, then off again on their crazy flight. I took a breath. "Maybe I feel too much."

I was glad when I finally heard the soft, regular sound of his breathing. He needed his sleep, and I needed to be alone with my thoughts. I lay awake, witnessing how the summer darkness in Alaska was never more than a murky dusk. At some point, I realized that the avalanches had stopped. The sun no longer softening the snowpack, the mountains finally went silent, and I was able to sleep.

We drove to Anchorage the next morning. Karl at the wheel, leaning forward in his seat as though he couldn't wait to get there and start our new life. Every time he thought of something to say, he took his eyes from the road to look at me.

"But we won't live in town," he said. "No way. We'll find a cabin to rent out in Chugiak or Eagle River. I don't mind commuting, and I'll bet you find a job close by."

I stared out the window. We were passing a huge area of dead trees, many of them no more than gray trunks. I remembered it from the drive up and had even asked Sara if there had been a fire. She explained the trees were all killed from flooding after the '64 earthquake. It looked so desolate to me now, like a nuclear holocaust. I missed Sara already and wished there was a way we could stay in Talkeetna. But there weren't many jobs there, and she was leaving for Mexico. Or Morocco, I thought, wishing for a sharp moment that I could go with her. I studied the sculpted peaks of the Chugach range, and soon I was fumbling the binoculars from under my seat and studying the shoulders of the biggest peak.

"Picking routes?" Karl asked.

"Always!"

He reached for my knee. "We'll do every one of them, I promise. Just think, this will be our backyard! What's that one called?"

I lowered the binoculars. Who needed Mexico or Morocco? "Pioneer Peak."

"That's exactly what we are! Pioneers! Pioneers of the Final Frontier!"

"Uh, this isn't *Star Trek*. Alaska is the *Last* Frontier."

"Whatever," Karl said with a laugh. He'd been in a great mood all morning, excited about our new life plans. He was a person who loved beginnings. New climbs, new towns, new people. Though it sometimes made me wary how he threw himself wholeheartedly into situations, I had to admit that it was one of the qualities I loved most in him.

We were passing Birchwood when Karl took the exit.

"Where are we going?" I asked.

"Let's have a look around."

We took a road into a neighborhood, crossed some railroad tracks, then turned onto a smaller gravel road where the houses were farther apart and more rundown.

"This is more like it," he said. "Some elbow room out here."

We were passing a long, rough driveway lined by a chain-link fence. A large cut of cardboard hung from a post with one word spray painted in black: *Puppies*.

Gravel pinged the undercarriage of the truck as Karl stepped on the brake and threw it in reverse. A mob of small, fluffy bodies was tumbling toward the chain link.

"Uh, oh," I said, grinning at Karl.

"We'll just take a look, okay?"

"Yeah, right."

But Karl was already stepping out of the truck. An old man in overalls came out of the dilapidated ranch-style home, and from the dog yard came a chorus of eerie howling.

"Good morning," he yelled over the almost musical canine sounds. The man ran his large, spotted hands up the sides of his overall bibs.

"We saw your sign. I'm Karl." They shook hands. "And this is Rachel, my fiancée."

"Well, congratulations! I'm Stan. You wanna get yourselves a puppy, eh?"

"You bet!" Karl said.

"I thought we were just looking?"

Stan chuckled, then motioned us to follow him into the dog yard. They looked like husky pups, each nearly identical to its littermates. I counted eight of them, rolling over and over in the dirt, yipping and growling.

Karl scooped one up and held it to his chest. The dog went stiff. Legs, tail, eyes froze in fear. He turned it over, and the dog cried in alarm. Karl replaced it gently back on the ground and went for another one, with much the same result.

I crouched to pet one, but the puppy moved back from my hand, wary.

"Have they been socialized much?"

"Well, some," Stan said, running his hands along his bibs again. "But they're only a few months old, and I like the owner to imprint on them, you see."

Karl placed a pup in my arms, and I felt that it wasn't only rigid but shaking. I put him down, and he scampered back to his littermates.

"How big will they get?" Karl asked.

"I have both Mama and Papa right here onsite. Come on and take a look?"

He led us to a tall, sleek husky, the mother. She was chained to her doghouse, and as we approached, she cowered.

"These here are working dogs, see," Stan said. "She's a beaut though, isn't she?"

"Yeah," Karl said.

"How about the father?" I asked.

"Well, him I gotta keep enclosed. Daddy can be a bit bull-headed, being almost pure like he is."

"Pure?" I looked to Stan, but he had already turned, motioning us to follow.

The enclosure was a six-foot chain-link fence covered by chicken wire. Pacing the short span was a huge gray animal with a long snout and yellow eyes. His legs were thick as bats, yet somehow gangly, giving the great animal a lean and rangy look. He was shedding his winter coat, and great tufts of it clumped from his haunches and throat. He moved along the fence on big splayed feet, turning again and again in the graceful, predatory manner of a shark. As we drew near, he lowered his enormous head and stared right into my eyes. Was he pleading with me? Condemning me? His yellow gaze pinned me to the spot.

"This isn't right," I said, turning to Stan. "That's a wolf."

"Almost pure." He stood back on his heels and offered a proud smile.

"He's beautiful!" Karl beamed.

I pressed my lips together. Was it right to domesticate a wild animal? Was it possible? "I don't know, Karl. I don't feel good about this. I mean, look at him. That's a wolf in a cage."

Stan laughed. "No, no, ma'am. It's a hybrid. I raise the best in the state."

"And the mom is all dog, right?" Karl cut in. "So the puppies are just a little bit mixed. They'll do okay as pets?"

"Sure, better than okay. You raise them from pups, and they're tame as can be. Mushers won't touch hybrids, say they're bossy and don't wanna work, but I like this guy. Now it's true, I can't run him with the boys on the team, and yes, okay, his main interests are eating and romancing the ladies, but there's something real neat about him. He came to me some years back, and I'd never give him up. In fact, I like him so much I breed him every spring. He makes the best-looking puppies in Alaska."

The animal's large ears twitched, and he turned his unnerving gaze on a tree. Halfway up, a squirrel began to chatter. "I need some time to think about this," I said. "Aren't they illegal?"

"Used to be this was a hell of a place." Stan removed his beaten red cap and quickly replaced it. "Now there's people everywhere flapping their mouths, regulating everything. Look, ma'am, these are fine dogs, and they make fine pets with a little tender loving care."

Karl threw an arm around me. "Why don't we take one more look at the puppies?"

We walked back to the dog yard, and I watched Karl handle one stiff pup after another. He picked up the largest one and cradled him against his chest. After a while, the pup began to kick and squirm, then relaxed and offered Karl's knuckle a tentative lick. "See honey, tender loving care."

I was still filled with the peculiar panic set off by the wolf's steady gaze. "Karl, I'm not sure about this. We're talking about taking in a wild animal. I mean, are wolves good with children?"

Karl and Stan laughed. "Ma'am, these are hybrids. They're really no different from my huskies. And like I said, you raise them from pups and they're your best friend."

Karl came close and held one of the litter for me to pet. His coat was soft and fluffy, and soon he began chewing on my hand with his needle-like teeth. Karl mouthed the word please, and I felt the panic within me begin to ease. If the father was only part wolf, then the puppies' blood was even more diluted. Maybe it wasn't so wrong.

"I guess he's gonna be somebody's pet," I said, "might as well be ours."

Karl kissed me on the cheek. "And we'll get him up in the mountains all the time! He'll have a great life with us."

As we drove away, the pup burrowed into my arms in fear, and by the time we turned onto the highway, he'd thrown up and peed.

"Good practice, *Mom*," Karl said, handing me his red bandana.

That night we returned to Eklutna to camp. We spent the day driving around Eagle River and Chugiak, looking at rentals that turned out not to accept pets. We even went into Anchorage to check out a couple, but as we drove past the strip malls and ugly urban landscape heading west into the city, we looked at one another and Karl turned the truck around. We promised each other that no matter what, we would not live in Anchorage.

Throughout the day, I had warmed up to the puppy. We named him Kiska after an island in the Aleutian chain and also for his penchant for giving kisses, toothy though they were. Both Karl's and my hands were scratched and bleeding, but we didn't mind. I was just glad he was acting more like a normal puppy.

By the time we got back to camp, it was nine o'clock. The sun, however, still shone down on us. "Let's take a hike," Karl suggested.

I grabbed the water bottle and daypack and looped one of the climbing ropes into a slip knot. As we started along the trail through the woods, I caught and leashed the pup. Down by the lake, several kayakers were just pulling out of the water. A small boy approached us. "Can I pet your puppy?"

"Sure. Why not?" Karl crouched and held Kiska still.

The boy ran his hand down the length of his coat, all the way to the tip of his tail. Kiska began to lick the boy's hand. When two other kids ran over to pet him, he cowered for a moment and then allowed his tail a little wag. Soon he was wagging his whole body, wiggling and squirming for the kids' attention. Karl and I looked at each other and smiled.

We continued on our hike, eventually letting Kiska run free. He bounded ahead, stopping only to investigate scents along the path. He disappeared for longer and longer stretches, and when we decided to leave the lakeside and take a mountain trail, we had to call him for nearly ten minutes before he came running back to us.

"It might take a while to find just the right place to live," Karl said, "but we'll find something. I know we will."

We were moving fast up the steep trail, the evening sun hot on my back. Sweat trickled from my forehead. "We need to start looking for work too."

"True. Although that doesn't sound like as much fun."

We continued to climb, the evening silence punctured by the sharp yips of a coyote down the valley. Another coyote answered from just above us on the mountain.

"Let's stop for some water," I said. "And something to eat. I'm starving."

I drew the bottle and some granola from my backpack, offering them to Karl. I sat down to rest on a flat section of trail. "Where's Kiska?" I asked. "We haven't seen him for a while."

"He's just having a good time." Karl took a seat next to me but whistled a few times. Still no Kiska, so I began to call him too.

"I'm getting really worried. Why would he just take off like that?"

"He'll come back," Karl said.

I packed up our snack and stood up. "Let's go look for him."

We spent an hour calling the dog before we decided to head down trail, hoping he made his way back to camp. He wasn't there either. A terrible thought sprang into my mind. "The coyotes got him. That's what happened."

"No," Karl said, throwing an arm around me. "No way. He's just exploring on his own."

I sat on the tailgate and felt tears coming on. "We should have kept him on the rope. He's just a puppy. We haven't even had him for a day, and we've already lost him."

"Look, I'll go back and look for him. You're tired. You gotta take care of yourself."

"I'm coming too. We'll split up. You go up the mountain, and I'll stick to the lake trail."

"It's going to be okay."

We didn't talk to each other on the hike back in but just called and whistled for the dog. We hugged each other at the mountain trailhead, agreeing to meet back at camp in an hour, and then we turned onto our separate paths. Clouds had moved in along with a light wind, quickly chilling me because of my damp T-shirt. I wished I'd brought my jacket. Coyotes yipped down the valley, and then a rumble like thunder startled me. Another avalanche high in the mountains nowhere near where we had been hiking. But now I was shivering, clutching my hands to my shoulders. Such dangerous country. So much out here that could take a life, especially a tiny thing like Kiska. I thought of what Sara said, how the number one lesson Alaska taught her was to be careful. My voice grew hoarse from calling the dog. How could Karl and I have been so stupid? And in just a few months' time we were going to have a baby? I sat down on a log as terrible thoughts crept over me. Maybe it was for the best, losing Kiska? He had wolf blood, wolf DNA, and how could we be sure he wouldn't hurt the baby? I imagined what my father would have to say about it, or even Sara, and I began to weep.

As I walked back, a twin sense of vulnerability and dread sawed away at me. It was peculiar and new to me, an in-between feeling. Not guilt or fear or horror but a combination of all three. I studied the ghostly peaks of the Chugach rising through the clouds far above me and shuddered. I vowed to myself that I would not start worrying about the bad things that might happen. Not only that, but I would take action to prevent them from happening.

When I reached our camp, Karl was sitting on the tailgate with a big smile on his face with Kiska sound asleep in his lap. "See? He's fine!"

I sprinted over to them. "Where did you find him?"

"Coming down the trail. He got a rabbit!"

I looked closer and saw that his gray muzzle was painted with blood.

"I had a hell of a time getting the carcass away from him. I had to put it in a tree and carry him away. He was so mad!"

I took a seat next to Karl and ran my fingers along Kiska's feathery coat. The pup roused a bit, stretched without opening his eyes, and settled back to sleep. I put a hand to either side of his head and scratched his ears and under his chin. He looked so sweet. Maybe he would be okay. "Let's promise each other that we're going to be more careful in the future."

"We won't lose him again."

Still cold, I rubbed my bare arms. "I should get my jacket." As I was slipping into my fleece, I noticed bright red streaks of blood along my arms. After a panicked moment, I figured out it wasn't my blood but Kiska's dead rabbit.

Yesterday I came across one of Karl's climbing ropes. In between nursing the baby and pacing the house with her, I spent pointless hours tying off knots, one after the other, like worry beads. Half-Hitch, Bowline, Figure-Eight. I couldn't stop picturing him, bound for Patagonia, as he disappeared through the flash of the airport doors, the bright neon colors of his backpack so familiar to me. He turned once and smiled and then was gone.

This morning I woke up surprised to be wedged between Stella and Kiska. Kiska usually slept by the front door, not coming into our room until six when he would stare at me with his amber eyes until I opened mine. It wasn't easy getting the dog and myself out of bed without waking Stella, and halfway down the stairs I turned back to pile pillows all around her to make sure she wouldn't fall out of bed. I let Kiska out into the small square of backyard and watched him circle the perimeter several times and pee all along the fence. I called him back in because if we left him out there for more than a few minutes, his thoughts turned to escaping.

He was a strange and difficult dog, and because I was home with Stella, all of his care fell to me. He needed a lot of exercise, but walking him was no easy task. He weighed over a hundred pounds and had a strong instinct to kill other animals, including neighborhood dogs, so I had to muzzle him and keep him on a choker. He'd nearly killed a black Lab in Eagle River, and we had to pay nearly $2,000 for the dog's vet bill. I felt bad about the life we made him live. He was only truly happy in the mountains, but I didn't get there very often these days, so he had to content himself running alongside Stella's stroller. I often found myself wishing we had an easy Lab or golden, but at least my worst fears hadn't proven true.

The afternoon we brought Stella home from the birthing center, I made Karl put the choker and muzzle on Kiska before we laid the baby on her play mat. Kiska cautiously sidled up to the squirming baby as though he feared stepping on her then gingerly sniffed her all over, and finally laid down at her side, his great head running the entire length of her body. From that moment on, he was devoted to her. There was something about the baby that calmed him, gentling the part of him that wanted only to run wild. I was surprised by this—and envious. The baby filled me with anxiety so much of the time. Her needs were so immediate and constant.

I heard Stella's morning cries start up. Kiska, always the first responder, loped past me as I headed to the bedroom. I wrapped Stella in her blanket and carried her downstairs to nurse by the big window in the darkened living room. It would be hours before the weak northern sun would rise. Kiska rested his long chin in my knee, and I thought, here we are, a couple of suburban misfits. Karl and I had never lived in a real house like this before, and though we'd vowed never to move to Anchorage, we'd ended up doing just that. Karl's commute was wasting too much time that he could've been spending with Stella.

I liked Anchorage more than I thought I would—the urban trails and mountain views and coffee shops. But I also found it ironic that the wilderness that brought us to Alaska was now one step removed. Maybe that was why I hadn't done a thing to make our house a home in the four months we lived here. Beige carpets, egg white walls, speckled gray cabinets in the kitchen and bathrooms. The colors were so bland I felt like I was being erased.

"Your tank full already?" I rocked Stella until she smiled and then I held her up to the picture window so she could look out at the new snow. The entire neighborhood was buried beneath it. She was mesmerized. My neighbor Tom, oblivious to us, was heaving shovelful after shovelful from his walkway. The day I met him, I introduced myself as a housewife, just to try it on and feel the full effect of the suburban horror. I thought he was joking when he said he was in the same trade. It was only partly true. He worked for an oil company way up on the North Slope—two weeks on and two weeks off—a job he hated. A Swiss immigrant, he came over on a whim to work on the pipeline in the '70s and never left. On his off time, he spent his days puttering in the garage or working on his truck or just standing in his driveway, looking thoughtfully at his house, waiting for his wife and two teenaged daughters to come home. Even up north where the winter days were short, there was still plenty of time to wade through.

To the east, a reddish glow was just barely touching the highest peaks. Flame-colored streaks appeared and spread through the darkened sky, slicing it open just above the ridgelines. The upper snowfields were catching the light, warming to shades of rose and tangerine. I felt a familiar surge in my chest, a primal thing, a call and response. I scratched Kiska's neck and wondered if that was what came over wolves when they howled at the moon. These sunrises were not rare up here on a clear winter day, and yet the sight of them always hit me like a once-in-a-lifetime opportunity—one that was slipping away. Soon the sun would be up and even though I'd watched the whole thing, I knew I would be left with the feeling that I somehow missed it all.

"Let's get Kiska to sing!" I bobbed Stella up and down and then began a long, slow warble. Stella clapped her hands and added her own thin voice to the chorus, until finally Kiska threw back his big head and unleashed the most heartbreaking of sounds. Stella and I both grew quiet as his howls filled the house with longing.

"That's enough! Shhh!" I held my hands around his snout. "Is your life that bad?"

I turned back to watch the sunrise, which had grown even more beautiful. But it was as though Kiska had struck a chord in me, and I couldn't shake it.

Outside, Tom had taken off his hat and was running his hands through his tufts of black hair. I considered yelling out the door so he wouldn't miss the sunrise, and in that moment he turned toward the mountains and dropped his shovel. Together, we watched until the peaks went white and the sky blue.

Karl said he'd never get used to this neighborhood, to living so close to the next house that you could lean out a window and touch it. But this morning I was comforted by it.

I fed Kiska and then ate some oatmeal while Stella sucked on orange slices. After breakfast, I bundled Stella and myself into our winter gear and carried her into the garage with the dog at my heels. Stella fought me as I strapped her into the car seat lashed to the big orange mountaineering sled, but she quieted when I pulled her outside into the frigid air. Kiska raised his muzzled nose, greedy for a scent. I took in a deep breath myself. It smelled like spruce needles and woodsmoke, and it felt good against my skin, like a splash of water.

Tom waved from his drive. "Cold enough for you?"

"Just about. Beautiful snow."

"It is," he agreed, extending his gloved hand for Kiska to sniff before smoothing back the dog's big gray ears. "Warmed up for a while there during the storm, but now the sun is out and it's freezing again."

I looked up the white trunk of a birch to its leafless black branches, unable to think of anything else to say. Kiska lay down in the snow and put his head between his paws.

"I'm tired of the cold," he went on. "Every winter I ask myself the same thing. Why am I still up north complaining? If we were smart, we'd head for Hawaii."

"If we were smart, we'd already be there." I'd never been to Hawaii, never wanted to go. But as soon as I said it, I couldn't help but imagine lying on the beach, warm winds on my skin, watching Stella roll naked in the sand.

Tom scooped up a shovel full of snow and held it at knee level. "Any news from Karl?"

"A couple of emails. I won't hear anything else for a while."

"When's he due back?"

"Three more weeks."

He raised his eyebrows. "That's a long haul."

I shrugged.

Dumping the snow into the growing pile in his yard, he looked down at Stella. "Go easy on your mom."

"Please," I said, "keep talking. She needs to hear this."

He crouched beside her. "Those are some eyes. Holy cow. What are they? Blue? Green?"

"Take your pick." I bent over her too. They really were something. Clear blue but for the touch of brown ringing her pupils. This combination kept her eye color in constant flux, like the mood ring I wore in college. Karl claimed she had my eyes, but it wasn't true. Mine were just flat blue.

"Well," Tom said, standing up. "Let us know if you need anything. It wasn't all that long ago my girls were this age." He smiled down at Stella and rested his hands one over the other on the shovel's handle and rocked it back and forth.

Stella whimpered from the sled. The sun shone but there was no warmth in it, and an icy wind had started up. I knew I should start running. Soon the baby would start crying, the tears on her face putting her at risk for frostbite. But I didn't want to leave yet. I reached down and dipped my mitten in the snow. My favorite type, light and airy, offered a deep, satisfying crunch under my boots. I wanted to roll in this snow, pile it over my legs, throw it in air, and scrub my face with it.

Stella cracked into a scream, and Kiska leapt to his feet. I lifted the sled rope over my shoulder. "Looks like it's time to go."

Tom dropped down next to the sled. "Hey there," he said, removing a glove and rubbing Stella's cheek while making a *tssking* sound with his tongue. I couldn't believe it. She went silent. Out of fear, no doubt, but at least she was quiet.

He smiled at her, deadpanned, then smiled once more. I saw how this expression had marked him. How the lines on his face were carved by kindness. It occurred to me that if there were some kind of emergency, I could leave Stella with him. I'd never thought about this before—what I would do if I couldn't be with Stella—but I was suddenly filled with relief.

He nodded over to my driveway. "Want me to shovel for you?"

"That depends," I said, grinning, unable to stop myself, "what will you charge me?"

He laughed, opened his mouth to say something, but just laughed again.

Later that night, I thought I heard Stella moaning. I sat up in bed and listened hard, but there was nothing. Squinting at the clock, I saw it was 3:00 a.m. I lay back down and stared at the Tibetan prayer flags crisscrossing our bedroom ceiling, squares of dyed cotton stretching out in a color sequence— blue, white, red, green, and yellow. Every night, the same. I woke up thinking Stella was crying, only to discover it was just a dog barking down the block or a police siren wailing past or, like tonight, nothing at all. She was six months old and still waking two or three times before morning, and though I always managed to nurse or rock her back to sleep within ten minutes, she left me wide-eyed and staring up at the flags.

Before the weather turned cold, Karl used to strap her in the Snuggly and take her on midnight runs around the neighborhood. It would always put her right to sleep, her cheek pressed against him, her little pink lips suckling the air.

Karl argued it was motion that did the trick. But I shook my head and said, "It's your heartbeat." I held my hand to his chest, just above her head, the thudding so alive under my touch I thought of Stella quickening in the womb. I loved to wrap my arms around him after these runs. The baby between us no longer an extension of myself, like during pregnancy, but an intersection of us both, where the two of us crossed.

I fell back asleep, and when I next opened my eyes to the prayer flags, a stone of guilt weighed within me. I'd dreamt of Tom. Nothing more than an embrace in his driveway, but such a vivid dream, the solidity of his body under all those layers of fleece and down.

Two days later I received a postcard, not of Antarctica but of Mayan ruins. Sara rather than Karl had sent it. She'd chosen to settle in Oaxaca for its language academy. Her money was quickly dwindling, but she claimed poverty beat out another winter in Alaska. *All the best to you and your spawn*, she wrote. I found myself hoping she would come back, but I didn't see any chance of it, especially not to Anchorage. Still, I was glad that I'd sent her our address last fall. I enjoyed keeping up with her travels, perhaps living vicariously through her. There were times in my own life where even a trip to the grocery store seemed too much of an undertaking.

That afternoon, Tom stopped by with his bright red travel mug and a paper sack full of powdered doughnuts. I glanced around the living room, embarrassed by the baby toys, books, and dirty dishes strewn about along with the dearth of furniture, including our milk crate coffee table. I've been to his house once, just after we moved to the neighborhood. It was a home of bright, airy rooms filled with heavy furniture, a kitchen with a red tiled floor and big iron pots hanging over the sink, and over the back door, a large clock with pictures of northern birds rather than numbers. It had all seemed so permanent.

I set the doughnuts on a milk crate, pushing away Kiska's inquiring snout. "Sorry, I should clean up a bit."

"It's fine. You have more important things to worry about." He took Stella from me and began to whisper *oopsie!* as he slowly dropped her to the floor. She stared at him with her unsettling gaze, the one that said she has seen all this before and was not impressed.

"This kid sure has a lot on her mind," he said.

"She takes after me."

I finished my decaf and most of the doughnuts. We spent the hour talking about natural disasters and moved through them all—volcanoes, hurricanes, earthquakes, wildfires. Everything except, by some tacit agreement, avalanches. I couldn't think of much else to talk about. A climbing rope hung in loops from the banister, and I uncoiled it and started working it through my fingers. I paused when I hit the frayed spot in the middle, the reason Karl left it behind.

"Is that your answer to knitting?" Tom asked.

"This one's for you." I made a loop and quickly wound the nylon into a series of twists before yanking the end. I dangled the rope in front of him. "Hangman's knot."

"Your mom has quite a talent," he said to the top of Stella's head. "Really, that's just charming."

"Okay, I'll do something a little more decorative."

He eased Stella onto her blanket on the floor, watching each twist I made in the rope. "Do you miss it? Climbing?"

My hands slowed. His question caught me off guard. "I don't know how to explain it to someone who doesn't climb."

"Give it a try."

I held the rope in my lap for a moment, rubbing my thumb over the damaged part. "Okay. Imagine what you love most in this world," I said. "Got it?"

"Yeah."

"Now imagine it's gone."

He nodded his head slowly. "I'm beginning to get the picture."

"So what was it? If you don't mind telling me."

"Oh, mine isn't an 'it,'" he said with a shrug. "It's a 'who.' Several of them, actually."

I lowered my eyes, tightness claiming my chest, and I busied myself with completing the knot.

"I swear it seems like only yesterday that Charlotte was this small." He said, placing his coffee mug on the crate. "I used to carry her around, like this."

He curled his empty forearm to his chest and held it there, his smile turning private and more beautiful, an expression for a child only he could see.

When he dropped his arm back down to his side, he cleared his throat and looked at the intricate loops of rope forming in my hands. "So what have you got there?"

A gentle pull on the ends of the line, and a double row of knots snap into perfect symmetry. I tied it bracelet-like around his thick wrist. "Chain sinnet."

It was early evening and Stella was at her worst, red faced and screaming in her car seat. The truck refused to start. I pressed my forehead against the steering wheel and thought, *If I could just get to the grocery store for something for dinner. If I could do this one simple thing.* Her cries echoed through the cab, bullets of sound ricocheting every which way. I was breathing fast, and yet I couldn't seem to catch my breath. What I needed to do was pull her into the front seat and nurse her right there in the cold truck, but instead I turned and begged her, "Please, just this once, stop crying. Please just stop. Please. Please."

She choked on an inhale, sputtered, and began to shriek in earnest. I turned onto my knees, reached over the front seat, planning to unbuckle her, but instead I found myself clenching my fists and pounding them on the roof as hard as I could.

"JUST SHUT UP! SHUT UP!"

Outside, the moon loomed big and yellow and very low in the sky. I rocked Stella inside my coat, rubbing her back, humming. She finally grew quiet, but all I could think about was getting through that night, and the next, and the next. I saw no end to it. None at all.

The following evening, I was on Tom's porch. Although a jump for a truck was a common enough request in cold country, I hadn't been able to knock on his door until now. My heart lobbed in my chest. Though the cold air burned my face, Stella, stuffed in her down suit, was blinking slowly and letting her eyes stay shut for moments at a time.

Nobody minded that I interrupted dinner. "I'll watch Stella," said Charlotte, the younger of Tom's daughters.

"And I'll watch Charlotte," said his wife, winking at me.

Tom pulled on his parka and followed me outside.

"This isn't the first time Yo has refused to start in the cold," I said. Calling the truck by name brought Karl to mind and the stone in my gut turned over.

I handed Tom the flashlight and cracked open the black box of jumper cables. When I popped the truck's hood, it squeaked as it always did in sub-zero weather. Tom reached for the cables, but I hugged them to my chest.

"You think I don't know my way around an engine?" I said. Truth was, I didn't know much beyond jumping a battery, but I knew I'd get a smile out of him. Taking hold of the thick clamps, I squeezed; negative-to-negative, positive-to-positive, the heavy metal teeth bit onto the nubs of the battery's terminals.

The thrill of the truck rumbling to life was quickly deflated by the thought of Tom going back in.

"Okay," he said, "I guess you're all set." He unclamped the cables and packed them back into the box. I moved closer to him between the exposed engines. He smiled quickly and turned, slamming close his front hood.

I took another step as a blue sedan moved slowly over the icy street, first past my house and then his. We were so close that the steam of our breath collided.

"We better get back," he said. He blew into his hands, then lifted his chin to glance down the block. I waited for him to look at me but he didn't. He blew into his hands again.

It occurred to me then that all of those beautiful lines of kindness could just as well have been carved by sadness, by opportunities he let slip away.

I pulled him into an embrace. It wasn't at all like the dream. He hugged me but just for a moment before he was pivoting backward from foot to foot. I didn't let go, not even when he whispered, "I'm sorry." I continued pressing myself against him until a familiar ache shot through my breasts; the milk letting down.

That night I couldn't sleep. My eyes were on the prayer flags once again, shifting through the sequence of colors. *Lung-ta.* That's what the locals called them. Windhorse. You were supposed to hang them from rooftops or bridges or mountain summits, anywhere the wind could hit them and free the prayers. But somehow they ended up here in the stillness of our room. Decorations.

I thought of the girl I bought them from outside a Buddhist shrine in Nepal. She indicated the wind in the flags by making a wavelike motion with her hand over and over again through the fabric. I tried to remember what she looked like, but it wasn't her face that came to mind. Instead it was the little girl from Talkeetna, the one who taught me how to pray.

I lurched upright in the bed. Stella turned over in her sleep, and I watched her fragile ribcage stand out as her lungs filled with air. I curled around her as she exhaled the puff of breath, still sweet from nursing. I became acutely aware of how very small she was. *This is it?* I thought. *This is all?* I pulled her closer into the hollow of my neck, this tiny child, this flesh and bone that I'd created out of nothing, as if by magic.

She stirred once again. I froze, but a low sound issued from way back in her throat and her lips parted, came together, parted. She was searching for me. She was always searching for me.

Would I trade places with Karl? With Sara?

I shut my eyes, and when I opened them, the prayer flags confronted me once again. Standing, I took hold of the stiff cotton and ripped them from the ceiling. They dropped lightly across the bed, the baby. I dragged the string of prayers down the steps and into the kitchen, then bunched them in my hands and kicked open the garbage can. I was so very tired, my body weighted with fatigue. Out the window, the snow came fast and hard. A shadow graced through the room. Kiska. He turned to face me, staring intently into my eyes.

"What?" I said aloud.

He continued boring into me, the uncanny gaze of a wild creature.

"I'm not feeding you yet."

With a patient air, he sat on his haunches, amber eyes still locked on mine.

"What do you want me to do? What?"

I finally broke free of him and found myself running the beautiful colors, one by one, through my hands. Blue, white, red, green, yellow. Windhorse.

I slipped out the front door, careful not to let Kiska follow. With the snow, the cold snap had broken. Wearing nothing but a T-shirt and underwear,

I carried the flags across the porch to the railing. Tying off a half-hitch, I stretched the prayer flags from the railing to the slender white trunk of our birch tree. I tied them high, as high as my arms could reach.

FREEZE-UP

Breakup in Anchorage was not a season in which you could store any faith. The ice sheets formed over puddles most nights, dirty clumps of snow waxed and waned along the curb, and then there was the occasional surprise snowfall. Karl had been gone a week when I glanced outside to see a quiet blizzard raging. I couldn't believe it, the first of May. By dawn our neighborhood was transformed into a silent tundra of rises and dips. Our truck was buried, and Stella's new red wagon gone altogether.

But two days later, the sun reigned over the city, throwing off heat like a midsummer day. Stella, Kiska, and I had been outside since lunchtime. Layers of fleece lay scattered around us, and we were down to T-shirts and sweats. Kiska's long tongue hung from his mouth as he panted in the sun. Though he was relaxed and lying down, I gripped his leash and kept scanning the neighborhood for any other animals. Bird, squirrel, cat, or dog set Kiska's wolf DNA into full tilt and turned him into a killing machine. I ran my hand along his thick winter coat, noticing he'd begun to shed it in the past week, leaving tufts of gray fur all over the house and our clothing.

"You're a pain in the ass," I whispered, as he licked my wrist and squinted his eyes into slits, a Kiska smile. "All you want to do is run wild."

I was alone again with Stella and the dog. Karl, in between contracts, had taken advantage of his time off by heading to Denali. We had a fight before he left.

"When is it my turn?" I yelled at him. "When do I get my life back?"

"You can do a climb when you quit nursing. I swear, I'll take care of Stella and you go do your thing."

I couldn't imagine that time would ever come. Or if it did, could I really leave her for weeks while I did a big trip? I didn't think so. "How can you keep taking off like this?" I asked. "When she's so young and changes so fast."

"I know. I hate doing this to you, to both of you. But I might not always get this kind of time off. And I just really want to try this route up the mountain."

I was angry, but at the same time I understood. If he was the one Stella so desperately needed all the time, I would take off at every opportunity as well.

Taking care of Stella and Kiska on my own had worn me down, but the nicer weather the last couple of days was lifting my spirits. I kicked off my clogs and plucked Stella's bright orange Crocs from her feet. She'd learned to walk a few days before, and I was cheering her progress as she followed a procession of carpenter ants across the driveway. Plopping down hard again and again, her rump was soaked with spring melt-off, yet each time she pushed herself forward onto her hands and straightened up with the determined balance of a surfer. Stella's face hung grim with resolve, eyebrows knitting together, lips pulling to one side. Karl's expression exactly. I wanted him here with me, marveling at this bright little soul we'd created together.

I was thinking of heading in and starting lunch when Kiska's big ears twitched and he set his gaze down the block. It was a police cruiser rounding the corner. Some part of me knew right away. Deep within me, I knew the cruiser would keep coming until it hit our driveway.

Karl had been gone for two weeks. Although I'd come to resent and dread his climbing trips, Stella never seemed to mind. At ten months old, she had no expectations at all. No disappointments, no yearning, no broken hearts. Her emotions were limited to just three, each rooted in the immediacy of now: rage, delight, and a catlike contentment that she slipped into while breastfeeding.

I watched the police car approach, slowly and stealthy. Kiska stood up and lifted his snout, trying to catch a scent of what was to come. The cruiser rolled quietly to a stop at our home, and I knew exactly what was happening. I knew.

"Ma'am," the officer said, his eyes dropping from mine to Kiska's, then back again. "Are you Rachel Burke?"

I nodded. Stella toddled over and wrapped herself around my leg. I lay a hand on her head.

"There's been an accident. Concerning your husband, Karl Burke."

Whatever I thought I knew was quite suddenly lost to me. "An accident?"

"He's passed away, ma'am."

"Where?" I dropped to a knee, held an arm around Kiska's neck. "Is he okay?"

"He's passed away ma'am. He was lost in an avalanche." The officer's voice grew as soft and intimate as a lover's.

"He's lost?" A buzzing began in my ears, and I shook my head again and again. "I don't understand what you're saying. Are they looking for him?"

"They found the body, ma'am."

His words kept coming, hushed and secret, words for my ears only. I grabbed Stella up in a too tight embrace, holding her like a shield to fend off the officer's tender voice. But Stella wouldn't have it. She kicked her legs, pushed against my chest and stomach until I had to loosen my grip. And when I let her go, my arms were empty. I had nothing to hold onto. I crouched on the blacktop, the flat of my palms pressing into the rough.

More voices whispered overhead, and then Tom the neighbor, crouched beside me. "What's happening?" I asked.

He took a knee and put his arm around me. "I'm so sorry. This is awful. But Karl is dead. He died."

I studied his eyes and saw that it was true. A feeling of terror beat within me, as if a large bird was trapped there by my heart.

"He was trying to help somebody," Tom said, "another climber. Karl was trying to help, but another avalanche hit, a big one, and they say he must have died quickly."

I thought I might get sick. I touched my forehead to the warm blacktop for a moment, then sat back up on my knees. "He wasn't asleep in his tent? When it hit, I mean."

"No. He was rappelling down to help someone."

"Are you sure?"

"Yes."

I was the one who'd been afraid of being taken out in my sleep, not Karl. Still, I clung to that small bit of consolation. But when Stella came back, pushing her way in between Kiska and me, the wings of my heart began to flap once again. I gave her a fierce hug.

"I know this road you're on," Tom said.

His voice brought me back, and I turned to look at him.

"I mean that I know this terrain. Losing someone."

Stella began to cry in my arms. I held her tighter.

And then Janet, Tom's wife, was there. She helped me up from the drive, plucked Stella up onto her hip, and called out several orders to Tom and the policeman. Soon after, she had me back in the house and on the futon with a hot cloth over my face. She put the baby into dry clothes and fixed her a bag of Cheerios and a sippy cup of grape juice, and told Tom to take Stella into the backyard. Every few minutes Janet would return with a new, hotter cloth and I lay hidden, breathing in the dark, wet, soap-scented air. Then she was gone for some time, and when she returned she handed me a sleeping pill and a cup of warm water, and sat at the end of the couch, watching over me with a mother's eye.

"Thank you," I said through the washcloth. I felt the pill rinse gently through me, a small current allowing me to stand back and away from the panic within me. "I don't know what I would have done. I didn't even understand the officer," I said.

"It was a shock."

I lay for a moment, my eyes shut against the warm soak of the washcloth. My mind drifted, then I murmured, "Tom said he knew this terrain. What did he mean by that?"

"Who?" she asked.

"Tom. He told me he knew this terrain."

"I see." She peeled the cloth from my face. "I better warm this up some." But she stood over me with an uncertain look on her face, wrapping the towel around her knuckles. "What Tom meant was that he understands." She took a slow breath and began unwrapping the towel. "You see, he was married before, and they had a baby, a little boy. His name was Peter, and he drowned. He was only two years old." She turned to go into the kitchen but looked back from the doorway. "Tom doesn't talk about him, and I've learned not to push. I think the key is to move on as best you can."

I stared back at her, wings once again brushing my heart. I was angry, but no words would come to me. After the door shut behind her, I didn't know if I said it or just thought it: *No.*

A busy week followed. The service had to be planned, arrangements made for friends and family making the long trip to Anchorage. I existed between two extremes, feeling either a panicked flapping of wings within me or a faraway drift, as if I was a flounder watching the progress of boats from way down on the ocean's floor.

I spent the day of the service in the flounder state. From far below the waves, I watched women crying, men shaking their heads in disbelief, Karl's alcoholic mother drinking big glasses of vodka and crying into wads of toilet paper and begging me to move to Pittsburgh. My father was there, saying little, appearing as lost and distant as I was.

Days earlier, I called a number in Mexico where I could leave messages for Sara, and I hadn't heard back from her. She must have moved on, maybe to Morocco for all I knew. Odd that I had such a need for her at that moment, a person with whom I'd only spent a few weeks. It occurred to me that friendship was no different than love. It wasn't the span of time that mattered but the depth of feeling.

Sleep that night was only possible because of Janet's little pills, but the next morning brought trouble. Four o'clock and I couldn't lie there for another second. I left Stella in the big bed, wedging pillows all around her. I let Kiska out into the yard and poured his kibble into his tin bowl and then called him into eat. The sound of the coffee grinder comforted me, as did the physical routine of placing the mesh filter into the basket, pouring water from the kettle slowly over the grounds. My father, asleep on the futon just off the kitchen, roused with the rich scent of coffee and settled himself quietly at the table. Kiska and my father, both silent company who helped center me. I dreaded my dad's departure later that day.

At the airport, he pulled me close, his faint lemon-scented aftershave emanating from within the deep folds of his neck, the same cologne he'd splashed on his skin every morning of my life, and the scent was so familiar to me that the flapping sensation resumed and tears sprang to my eyes.

"I don't know what to do," I whispered into his worn shirt collar.

He nodded his head and then handed me a white envelope. Being broke was not a new experience for me. Until a year ago, Karl and I were living in our truck. I knew poverty would be a different thing now that I had Stella and we were alone, but lack of money wasn't what scared me. I couldn't articulate my fear, so I just stuffed the check into my jacket pocket.

"Thanks."

"It'll all work out," my father said in his broken old man's voice. "You'll see."

I spent the summer looking for work and a good daycare for Stella, and by late August, I made a list of items to put on Craigslist. We didn't have much besides climbing gear. No TV, no nice jewelry, our stereo too old to be worth anything. I knew there was no way we could keep the house. I wrote our address on the list under my climbing harness, and then I took one of Janet's sleeping pills and the world ended for a while.

Sara sent me a letter with her new address in Guatemala. She found a summer job teaching English and claimed they paid her in tortillas. She didn't have a phone, but we exchanged several letters, and in one she gave me a lead on a job. She once worked at a café in Eagle River that offered health insurance after three months, and she said she'd write to the owner, also a climber, and put in a good word for me. I received a call the very next week offering me an interview, and by the following day, I had the job.

The day we were to move to Eagle River, I woke up to the sound of a woman screaming. I lurched out of bed to the open window and listened, heart pounding. There was another scream, but it came from the sky overhead. I realized it was some sort of bird, and I crawled back under the warm down blanket and held Stella's warm body close to my racing heart.

After breakfast, I began to clean house and pack up, making a pile out on the porch of our Craigslist items. Tom walked over from his driveway; his hands plunged deep into his jeans' pockets.

"Gonna be getting cold soon. Freeze-up's maybe a month away," he said, hefting a box from my arms and setting it on the bed of the truck. "I feel bad," he said, shifting his weight in the restless way horses do. "You having to clear out like this."

I shrugged. "That's life."

"But I'm sure your new place is nice."

"No," I said. "I'm renting a trailer, Tom. A trailer with brown carpet. It's not even big enough for Kiska to stretch out in." I shook my head. "But it's close to where I work, and cheap, with a good view of the mountains. It's got a big yard for Stella, and plenty of mountains for Kiska. So who cares if we're trailer trash now?" I said with a weak laugh.

"No," he said. "No way. You'll make it good. Soon enough."

I shrugged and looked up at the sky. Overhead, trees swayed in the wind; green leaves fluttered and rustled. I grew dizzy watching them, and I recalled a strange event from waking up that morning. It hit me suddenly like dreams sometimes do. "This morning when I woke up," I said, "I thought I heard a woman screaming."

Tom was coiling a tangled climbing rope for me, but he stopped now and gave me a careful look. "*Was* it a woman screaming?"

"No," I said.

His expression relaxed. Eyebrows raised and furrowing his broad forehead, he waited for an explanation.

"It was some kind of bird," I continued. "Flying over the house."

"Loons," he said, brightening.

"I didn't know there were loons in the city."

"We have a pair that stops over every year at the end of summer. They fly right over our neighborhood going from the lagoon downtown to the bog by the airport."

Stella tottered across the drive and grabbed onto my leg. I picked her up onto my hip. "How do you know it's the same two birds?" I asked.

"Loons are territorial and they mate for life." He glanced at me, a flicker of apology in his eye, before pressing ahead. "They stick to the same migration routes. God, I love hearing their calls. Sometimes it sounds like laughing, like they're just laughing away at some joke. And sometimes they howl, just like wolves. Sounds like their hearts are breaking."

"Well this morning that bird was screaming. Just like a woman."

I sat down on the blacktop and leaned against the big rear tire of the truck. I tilted my head back, the midday sun blinding me so that Tom was no more than a shadow.

He eased himself down beside me. His broad shoulder against mine felt solid as packed earth.

"You know what I'm worried about, moving to the mountains?"

"What?"

"From my trailer, I'll have a perfect view of Denali. Every single clear day."

"It's hard, isn't it?"

"Yes, it is. And it seems to keep getting harder rather than easier."

"True. Even still for me, and it's been a lot of years, now." He nodded his head. "See, I was married before. When I was young. I'd just come over from Switzerland to work the pipeline and met a girl, and that was it. I stayed. We had a baby, a little boy named Peter, and he drowned."

"I'm sorry."

"Me too."

"I don't really know what else to say."

"Me neither."

Stella, jealous for my attention, pushed herself into my arms. I began to rock her, and she shut her eyes against the bright sun. Soon she was asleep. *What would it be to lose her?* I thought. But there was no feeling in either the question or response.

Tom gazed down at Stella. Her head turned to one side, her full lips suckling three of her tiny fingers. "She's so peaceful." His eyes glassed over as he watched her.

I looked at her too.

After some time, he said, "I think that's what you'll have to do with your mountain."

"What?"

"Find peace."

After I moved, Tom and Janet called to check in every few days. Then in late September, Tom came into the café where I worked. His skin was ruddy from the autumn air.

"On my way to the valley," he said. "I got a moose last week, and it's just too much for us." He motioned out the window to his pickup. I could make out a large red cooler in the back. "There's some salmon, too."

"Thanks," I said. "But Tom, I don't have a freezer in the trailer. Even the fridge is tiny. But I do appreciate the thought."

He ducked his head and turned to me. "I didn't think about that. Guess I wasn't thinking at all." He drummed his fingers on the counter. "Well, at least you could take enough for this week. It's nice and fresh."

"Okay," I said. "I'll do that."

We stood for a moment in silence. The café was empty, which was strange for early afternoon.

"How's Stella liking her new home?" he asked.

"She loves it. And she likes her daycare. I found this co-op thing, just moms taking turns watching the kids."

"That's great. And how about Kiska?"

"Oh, he's still a pain. I have to keep him in a crate in the truck while I'm working. But every chance I get, I put Stella in the pack and hike into the mountains with him. Even then I have to keep him on a rope."

"And yet you keep him?"

"Are you kidding? There's no way I could take him away from Stella. He'd find his way back to her." I turned to stack some coffee mugs along the back shelf. "And you know what? He makes me think about Karl, or maybe how Karl and I were together. Before the baby, I mean."

"And how were you?"

"Stupid," I said as I turned back to him. "And so incredibly young. I can't believe it was just a couple years ago. But I guess I like thinking about that time in our lives."

He nodded. "And what about you? How are you doing out here in the wilderness?"

I thought for a while before I answered. People were constantly asking me how I was doing, and my reply was as automatic as it was untrue: fine. Now I wanted to be honest. It wasn't an easy question. "Still here," I finally said. "Breathing."

"Good, that's good," he said. "Breathing can take a lot of work sometimes."

He reached across the counter to hold both my hands in his. I was glad there were no other customers in line, and I was able to simply stand and accept his warm touch. A moment came in which I should have removed my hands, but I didn't. I let that time pass. I didn't look at him but at a white rag soaking in a small bucket of bleach and water on the counter. My hands were tense in his. I didn't know how to let go. A customer came through the door then, the bells above it jingling, and a cold, fresh draft replaced the bleach scent stinging the air, and still I held on.

"I have no idea how to go on," I whispered.

He nodded and leaned closer. "What do you mean?"

My breath caught high in my chest. "Stella," I said.

"What about her?"

I couldn't think of how to answer him. Words just wouldn't come. Then my boss, Amanda, came out from the kitchen. She threw an arm around me.

"Why don't you go ahead and take a good long break," she said. "It's slow today. I can handle it on my own for a while."

I let Kiska out of his crate in the back of the truck for a while and gave him some water. Then Tom drove me to the trailer so I could put up the moose meat. Rather than go in, though, we sat on the tailgate of his truck. The strong breeze from the morning had eased, and the sun, though weaker now in late September, felt warm and liquid against my skin.

Tom didn't say anything, and for that I was grateful. We sat shoulder-to-shoulder for a long time in the sunlight. And then Tom turned to me and said, "Back at the café, you said you didn't know what to do about Stella. What did you mean?"

I shrugged and shut my eyes against the sun.

"Come on. You afraid of raising her alone?"

"No, not exactly. I mean, of course I am, but that's not what's really getting to me. Sometimes," I opened my eyes to look at him now, "I'm afraid that she knows things about me. Like she can sense things."

"What things?"

"Things that are missing in me."

"Like what?"

I raised my hands and dropped them. "Everything."

He thought about this for a while, and then nodded slowly. "I think I know what you mean. You're walking and talking, but there's nothing," he tapped on his chest, "here. It's called grief."

I stayed silent. How could I explain I was like this before Karl died?

The sunlight shone such a warm shade of gold that it wasn't warmth so much as the color itself entering my skin and hair. It began to have an effect on me, to ease something in me. "Everything is missing," I said. Oddly, it felt good to say those words in all that golden light. "Everything," I said louder.

Tom shrugged. "You know what the hardest part for me was, losing my child? I constantly had the feeling that I had to go to him, to hold him, to comfort him, but that was impossible, and I just couldn't get my mind around it. Who would comfort him, I kept thinking? Who's holding him now? It hurt me, and I mean physically, it hurt."

"And how did you move on?"

"To be honest," he shook his head, "I'm not sure I have. There's a part of me that's still . . . back there."

Just then, a faraway calling trailed up the valley. Like a breeze or a fluttering of leaves, the noise came to us. Tom squinted his eyes skyward and lifted a hand as a sun shield. I did the same.

"Canadians," he said. "Canadian geese. Freeze-up will be here soon."

We were close, drawing together as the geese flew overhead. They were scattered in a wavering mass across the sky, filling the air with a cacophony of deep-throated honking. There were so many birds they blocked out the sun as they passed. I held my breath watching them go, and when they were just over us the geese pulled into a tighter and more resolute diamond, each bird sharpening its position in the whole. It took less than ten seconds for the mess of individual birds to pour into a streamlined formation above our heads. And just as quickly, the sky emptied of geese. They became distant points on the horizon and then nothing at all. Tom and I were left alone staring into the bright blue silence.

We turned to each other in disbelief, and I found that I'd taken up his hand. It was calloused hard as plastic at the palm. He pulled me against his chest and held me for a long time before we moved into the trailer. We were unhurried with one another. When I lay under him, both of us completely undressed, what I felt wasn't passion but a deep sense of sadness. His hands on my hips, his lips on my breasts, every touch stirred a deeper layer of pain.

We didn't talk during the drive back to my truck, not until I opened the door to leave.

"I've got to consider my family in all of this," he said. "I need time to think, to make it all right for everyone. I'll call you soon and we'll figure it out."

I slid off the seat and out the door. "Don't."

I picked up Stella from the co-op and bundled her against the sunset chill in a thick fleece jacket and woolen mittens, every day one day closer to freeze-up. I took her down to the small lake a few blocks from our trailer.

The sky had turned to iron, a solid mass of low clouds the same color as the lake water. She strode to the edge and dipped her mitten-clad hand into the cold water, her eyes shot back to me in surprise.

"Cold," I said. "That's cold water. Brrr."

"Brrr," she said back to me. "Brrrrr." And then she stuck both her feet into the lake, water spilling over the tops of her boots. She began to cry.

I hurried over to her, lifted her out of the water and took her boots off, one by one, pouring water from each. I peeled off her wet socks and replaced them with my mittens. Stella cried and cried.

"It was just cold, that's all," I said.

She continued to cry.

"Look, you're going to have to toughen up a bit. It's okay. It was just cold, that's all."

"No!" she yelled at me, angry now. She stood up and strode back to the lake, one mitten falling off. "Brrr!" she howled out at the water. And then she threw a look back at me that was pure Karl, eyes squinting in fury, and I thought I'd start crying too. But I cracked into a smile, and then I laughed and laughed.

"That's right, Stella! Stand up for yourself!"

She studied me, unsure of my change in mood. Then she began to laugh as well. I pulled her close and folded her body against mine, her legs were getting so long, and I pressed my lips into her soft curls until I could feel the surprising firmness of her skull. She didn't protest or struggle against me, and we stayed like that for some time. To the east all was dark, to the west the dull bruise of sunset continued to sink, but I shut my eyes and felt love flocking within me from all directions, swooping and tightening and pulling together, and I thought I should take Stella home and cook her something good—spaghetti, that was her favorite—and I knew that in one more moment I would do just that.

The next day at work I'd just finished cleaning the windows when I saw a backpacker get off the Anchorage bus and trudge up the hill toward the café. Her face was deeply tanned behind big sunglasses, and she wore a green bandana over her hair, pirate-style.

"No way," I said aloud. Three customers glanced up at me. "That's Sara!"

I ran out the door and hugged her in the parking lot.

"What are you doing back in Alaska?"

"I got sick of nice weather," she said, dropping her backpack on the pavement. "Every single morning, beautiful warm sunshine. Always the same. I miss winter, believe it or not."

"Well, you've come to the right place, darling!" I hoisted her pack onto my back. "You want some coffee?"

"Yes, ma'am!"

As we walked into the café, something occurred to me. I turned and gave her a weak smile. "Are you on your way to Talkeetna, then?"

"No, I don't think so. Too many ex-boyfriends in that town. I figured I'd stick around here for a while and get to know that little troublemaker of yours."

I set her backpack behind the counter, grinning at her. "Don't say I didn't warn you! And you're welcome to stay with us, by the way. It's just a trailer, and the dog takes up most of it, but you can stay as long as you can stand it."

"Sounds great! Thank you!"

"You don't need to say thanks, not after all you've done for me."

Soon we were hiking the trail that rose from my place up into the Chugach. Stella, usually impatient in the back carrier, happily peered over my shoulder, eyes glued to Sara. Kiska, too, seemed thrilled by her presence, not straining on the leash to run ahead, but frolicking by Sara's side, thrusting his wet nose over and over into her hand.

"I don't know what you were talking about. This crew seems pretty okay to me," she said.

"I think this is the dog and baby version of the honeymoon phase."

We stopped on a switchback of the trail to take in the view below. The birch trees had just begun to turn, dotting the green river valley below with bright yellow. I pulled a graham cracker from my pocket and held it level with my ear until Stella's hand closed over it. Sara and I passed a Nalgene bottle of water back and forth and listened to the sound of the wind in the trees.

"I have to say I'm surprised to see you back here," I said, eyes still searching the valley below.

"Why? You're still here, aren't you?"

"I pretty much got stuck here. You could go anywhere in the world and then keep on going."

She thought about this for a minute. Below us, but high over the river, two ravens soared and tumbled as they played in the currents of wind.

"I was in Mexico," she said, "and my plan was to hang in Baja for a while. I spent most of the day at the beach, and when I went back to my hostel, I was tired out. I was laying in the hammock drinking a pilsner when an old man shuffled by. He was barefoot, all hunched over with a huge sack of sticks on his back. He smiled this big toothless grin at me, and hollered, 'How beautiful it is to do nothing and rest afterward!'"

I laughed.

"But you know what? I got tired of it. Traveling around aimlessly, making friends one day, just to say good-bye the next. That old man with the bundle of sticks made me realize how homesick I was." She looked from Kiska to Stella and then to me. "The next day I left for Alaska."

That evening as the sun set, we made a campfire for the first time out in front of the trailer. It was chilly, the cold air blending with the scent of our woodsmoke and the season's wet leaves. We were all tired from our hike in the mountains, and Kiska lay with his great head in Sara's lap. Stella, still shy, remained in my arms but kept her eyes trained on Sara. We sipped hot chocolate from thick mugs as we listened to the wind strip leaves from the birch and alders. From our high vantage point, we watched three mountains grow more distinct against the purpling sky: Foraker, Hunter, and biggest of all, Denali. Sara looked as though she was going to speak but then simply nodded at me. We sat in silence until the sky went black.

"The gods have gone to sleep," she said.

I looked down at Stella, her eyes closed, eyebrows knit just like her father's in sleep. On her, the look was one of peace rather than worry. "Good night, gods." I said it quietly, careful not to wake the baby.

ACKNOWLEDGMENTS

Many people aided and abetted me in creating this book, and I could not have produced it without their help, support, and encouragement. In 2015, the Rasmuson Foundation granted me an Individual Artist Award, making it financially possible to complete my manuscript of this collection of stories. The staff at University of Alaska Press has been fantastic. Much thanks to Laura Walker, Elizabeth Laska, Dawn Montano, Krista West, and Nate Bauer. Peggy Shumaker encouraged this project from the start; she is a great blessing to the Alaska literary scene. I would also like to thank the entire English Department at the University of Alaska Anchorage for their enthusiasm for my writing. Ron Spatz, Sherry Simpson, and Arlitia Jones offered feedback on many original drafts of these stories, which helped me immensely

For many years, Vered Mares of VP&D House has been a wonderful friend and editor, and she continually inspires me in her literary pursuits. Writer Lucian Childs was never too busy to lend me a hand with this manuscript, for which I am forever in his debt. Much thanks to writers Mei Mei Evans, Liz Meredith, Rich Chiappone, Kris Farmen, Mike Burwell, Sandra Klevin, and Buffy McKay. Jeremy Pataky and 49 Writers are such a gift to Alaska, and I can't imagine literary life in this state without them. Furthermore, I wish every good thing for hard-working Rachel Epstein of the University of Alaska Bookstore for her wonderful support of local literary arts. Indra Arriaga, who painted the beautiful cover art, is not only a friend but a true inspiration to me.

Lastly, thank you to my large and loving family. My parents always encouraged us not just to read but to live our lives within the context of literature. So to my parents and many siblings, all booklovers, thank you. And I am one lucky woman to have such a wonderful life partner, my husband, John, along with our three highly entertaining daughters, Kate, Lily, and June, who fill our home with laughter.

ABOUT THE AUTHOR

Martha Amore teaches writing at the University of Alaska Anchorage. She achieved her master of fine arts from the University of Alaska Anchorage in 2009 and has published stories in a number of journals and magazines, including *Room,* Canada's oldest feminist literary journal. In 2013 VP&D House published her novella in the anthology *Weathered Edge: Three Alaskan Novellas.* In 2015 she won a Rasmuson Individual Artist Award to complete her manuscript of short stories, *In the Quiet Season.* In 2016 Martha Amore and coeditor Lucian Childs were contributing editors of the University of Alaska Press anthology *Building Fires in the Snow: A Collection of Alaska LGBTQ Short Fiction and Poetry,* which was a finalist for a LAMBDA Literary Award. She is currently at work on an interdisciplinary PhD through the University of Alaska Fairbanks.